TARASOFF
AND BEYOND:
LEGAL AND CLINICAL CONSIDERATIONS IN THE TREATMENT OF LIFE-ENDANGERING PATIENTS

Revised Edition

Leon VandeCreek, PhD
Department of Psychology
Indiana University of Pennsylvania

Samuel Knapp, EdD
Harrisburg, Pennsylvania

Professional Resource Press
Sarasota, Florida

Published by
Professional Resource Press
(An imprint of Professional Resource Exchange, Inc.)
Post Office Box 15560
Sarasota, FL 34277-1560

Printed in the United States of America

Copyright © 1989, 1993
by Professional Resource Exchange, Inc.

The copy editor for this revision was Patricia Hammond, the
managing editor was Debbie Fink, the graphics coordinator was
Laurie Girsch, and the cover designer was Bill Tabler.

The views expressed in this guide do not necessarily represent
those of the Pennsylvania Psychological Association.

Library of Congress Cataloging-in-Publication Data

VandeCreek, Leon.
     Tarasoff and beyond : legal and clinical considerations in the
treatment of life-endangering patients / Leon VandeCreek, Samuel
Knapp. -- Rev. ed.
          p.   cm. -- (Practitioner's resource series)
     Includes bibliographical references (p.   ).
     ISBN 0-943158-91-5 (paper)
     1. Mental health laws--United States. 2. Psychotherapists--Legal
status, laws, etc.--United States. 3. Confidential communications-
-Physicians--United States. I. Knapp, Samuel. II. Series.
KF3828.V36   1993
344.73'041--dc20
[347.30441]   93-6607
                                                                    CIP

PREFACE TO THE SERIES

As a publisher of books, cassettes, and continuing education programs, the Professional Resource Press and Professional Resource Exchange, Inc. strive to provide mental health professionals with highly applied resources that can be used to enhance clinical skills and expand practical knowledge.

All the titles in the *Practitioner's Resource Series* are designed to provide important new information on topics of vital concern to psychologists, clinical social workers, marriage and family therapists, psychiatrists, and other mental health professionals.

Although the focus and content of each book in this series will be quite different, there will be notable similarities:

1. Each title in the series will address a timely topic of critical clinical importance.

2. The target audience for each title will be practicing mental health professionals. Our authors were chosen for their ability to provide concrete "how-to-do-it" guidance to colleagues who are trying to increase their competence in dealing with complex clinical problems.

3. The information provided in these books will represent "state-of-the-art" information and techniques derived from both clinical experience and empirical research. Each of these guide books will include references and resources for those who wish to pursue more advanced study of the discussed topic.

4. The authors will provide numerous case studies, specific recommendations for practice, and the types of "nitty-gritty" details that clinicians need before they can incorporate new concepts and procedures into their practices.

We feel that one of the unique assets of the Professional Resource Press is that all of its editorial decisions are made by mental health professionals. The publisher, all editorial consultants, and all reviewers are practicing psychologists, marriage and family therapists, clinical social workers, and psychiatrists.

If there are other topics you would like to see addressed in this series, please let me know.

Lawrence G. Ritt, Publisher

ABSTRACT

The legal and clinical problems in treating life-endangering clients were highlighted in the case of *Tarasoff v. Regents of the University of California* (1976). Although the *Tarasoff* decision is the most famous court case dealing with life-endangering clients, other common-law cases and statutory rules also regulate the treatment of life-endangering clients.

This guide discusses the *Tarasoff* decision and subsequent related court decisions and their legal and clinical implications. The guide focuses primarily on the management of homicidal patients. In addition, the authors extend their discussion to the management of suicidal patients and child-abusing parents. To a lesser extent, other topics are discussed, including legal responsibility in dealing with AIDS patients, incompetent drivers, patient disclosures of past crimes, and therapist liability for wrongful civil commitments. Although not intended as a comprehensive treatment manual, this guide discusses clinical interventions and considerations that will minimize liability risks and, at the same time, provide quality treatment for patients.

In this revision, the authors include information and references to the most recent research findings and court cases.

TABLE OF CONTENTS

PREFACE TO THE SERIES   iii

ABSTRACT   v

INTRODUCTION   1

THE FACTS OF THE *TARASOFF* CASE   2

    Dissenting Opinions   7
    Background on Duty to Protect   7
    Living with *Tarasoff*   9

SUBSEQUENT CALIFORNIA CASES   10

APPLICATION OF *TARASOFF* IN OTHER STATES   13

    Application to Outpatient Settings   13
    Negligent Release of Patients   15
    Court-Ordered Releases   18

FAILURE TO CONTROL OR COMMIT   18

    Failure to Commit Before *Tarasoff*   18
    Failure to Commit After *Tarasoff*   19
    Outpatient Commitment   22
    Immunity Laws   22

LIABILITY FOR SUICIDES   24

  Inpatient Suicides   25
  Outpatient Suicides   27

REFUSALS TO EXPAND *TARASOFF* RULES   30

AIDS AND THE DUTY TO PROTECT   32

CLINICAL MANAGEMENT IN
LIGHT OF *TARASOFF*   36

STATUTORY REMEDIES TO *TARASOFF*   40

OTHER LEGAL ISSUES WITH
DANGEROUS PATIENTS   42

  Abandonment   42
  Duty to Consult or Refer   44
  Wrongful Commitment   45
  Application of Section 1983 of the
    Civil Rights Act   47

PROSECUTING PATIENTS   49

MANDATORY REPORTING LAWS   50

  Child Abuse   50
    Incentives and Penalties under Mandatory
      Reporting Laws   51
    Recent Problems with Mandated Reporting   53
    Clinical Management of Potential Abuse Cases   54
  Adult Abuse   55
  Incompetent Drivers   55
  Disclosures of Past Crimes in Court   56

SUMMARY   57

REFERENCES   59

TARASOFF AND BEYOND: LEGAL AND CLINICAL CONSIDERATIONS IN THE TREATMENT OF LIFE-ENDANGERING PATIENTS

INTRODUCTION

Psychotherapists find few situations as stressful as dealing with life-endangering patients. Therapists may be called to the emergency room of a hospital late at night to evaluate a prospective patient accompanied by the police or relatives. The examination may be made under difficult circumstances. The police may present their concerns in a demanding manner, and the relatives may lie blatantly to rid themselves of the patient. In addition, the patient may be angry, confused, or afraid to communicate.

In another context, the psychotherapist may be working with a voluntary outpatient, trying to defuse hostile and aggressive feelings and fantasies. The patient's anger or disorganization may become so severe that the psychotherapist fears that a life may be endangered.

When working with life-endangering patients, the psychotherapist changes roles, from an ally trying to activate the healthy aspects of the person to an agent of social control who determines that an intended victim must be warned, or that the patient must submit to an evaluation for an involuntary commitment.

In one sense, the more severely disturbed patients are the easiest to evaluate. The dangerousness of their acts and the degree of mental disorganization leave no doubt as to the proper decision. Other decisions are harder. When do threats become so severe that it is necessary to warn the intended victim? When does a suicidal gesture become severe enough to qualify as a suicidal act? How long can a person go without eating before it qualifies as neglect of self?

No psychotherapist - no matter how competent - can make these decisions with complete accuracy and foresight. Despite their extensive study of psychopathology, mental health professionals are often limited in their ability to predict dangerousness. They may find themselves in a double-bind. The failure to warn an intended victim may mean that a life is endangered. Conversely, that warning may alienate the patient from psychotherapy and increase the very danger that the psychotherapist was trying to avert.

These dilemmas were brought into sharp focus in 1976 when the California Supreme Court concluded that psychotherapists have a duty to protect potential victims from dangerous patients (*Tarasoff v. Regents of the University of California*, 1976). A few commentators and therapists welcomed the court's conclusion as an endorsement of their current practices or ethical standards (e.g., Leonard, 1977). Nevertheless, the majority of mental health practitioners and scholars were shocked, angered, and frightened by the court's entry into the exclusive sphere of professional judgment.

The courts have been reluctant to enter the domain of professional practices, preferring to defer to the experts in those fields. The *Tarasoff* court concluded, however, that important legal principles were in conflict. The court believed that it had to enter the mental health field to correct an imbalance between the rights of psychotherapy patients to confidentiality and the rights of potential victims to safety from assault by these patients.

Subsequent court decisions in California and in other jurisdictions have sometimes clarified and sometimes muddied the issues. Nonetheless, it is possible to glean some general principles from these court cases, which together have forced the mental health professions to address the legal and clinical problems of treating life-endangering patients.

THE FACTS OF THE *TARASOFF* CASE

Prosenjit Poddar was born in Bengal, India, into the Harijan ("untouchable") caste. In September 1967, he entered the University of California at Berkeley as a graduate student and took up residence in the International House. In the fall of 1968, he attended folk-dancing classes at the International House, where he met and fell in love with a young American woman, Tatiana (Tanya) Tarasoff. Poddar persisted in courting Tarasoff, and he apparently misinterpreted her friendliness (including a New Year's Eve kiss) as a sign of deep affection and commitment. However, Tanya did not return his affections. She told him that she was involved with other men and did not want an intimate relationship with him.

Poddar underwent a severe emotional crisis after Tanya rebuffed him. He neglected his appearance, health, and studies. He often stayed alone, spoke disjointedly, and wept. He saw Tanya only occasionally during the spring of 1969. At times he tape-recorded parts of these conversations (apparently without her knowledge) in an attempt to understand why Tanya did not return his love.

During the summer of 1969, Tanya went to Brazil and Poddar's emotional health began to improve. At the suggestion of a friend, Poddar sought mental health treatment at the Cowell Memorial Hospital, an affiliate of the University of California at Berkeley. He was initially interviewed by a psychiatrist, Dr. Stuart Gold, and then started psychotherapy with a psychologist, Dr. Lawrence Moore.

During the session of August 18, 1969, Poddar confided to Moore his intent to kill Tanya when she returned from Brazil. Moore took the threats seriously. On August 20th, he consulted with Dr. Gold and Dr. Yandell, the assistant director of the department of psychiatry. They agreed that Poddar should be involuntarily committed to a psychiatric hospital. Moore then asked the campus police to pick up Poddar and to proceed with commitment procedures. Moore stated that he would follow up the conversation with a letter of diagnosis.

In his letter to the campus police, Moore stated that Poddar was undergoing an acute and severe paranoid schizophrenic reaction and that he was a danger to others. Moore also stated that Poddar appeared rational at times, but quite psychotic at other times.

The campus police officers detained Poddar and talked to him. They did not commit him, however, because he appeared rational and promised to avoid Tanya. After the commitment attempt failed, Poddar discontinued therapy. Subsequently, Dr. Harvey Powelson, the director of the department of psychiatry, learned of the foiled arrangement to commit Poddar. He re-

3

quested that the police chief return Moore's letters, ordered Moore to destroy his therapy notes, and requested that no further attempts be made to commit Poddar.

The attempt to commit Poddar occurred only 2 months after the enactment of California's new commitment law, the Landerman-Petris-Short Act. Consequently, neither the mental health professionals nor the police were experienced with the procedures required by the new commitment law. They also may have been uncertain about how the courts would interpret the new law. In fact, according to the new law, the city police, not the university police, should have picked up Poddar and transported him to a medical facility for an emergency psychiatric evaluation.

That fall, Tanya returned from Brazil, unaware of the danger to her. Meanwhile, Poddar persuaded her brother to share an apartment with him only a block away from Tanya's residence. On October 27, 1969, Poddar went to Tanya's house to speak to her. Tanya refused to speak with him, but Poddar insisted. Tanya screamed, whereupon Poddar shot her with a pellet gun. Tanya fled the house, but Poddar apprehended her and repeatedly and fatally stabbed her with a kitchen knife. Poddar then returned to Tanya's house, where he called the police.

At the trial, Poddar's attorneys argued a defense of diminished capacity. They produced a psychologist and three psychiatrists who stated that Poddar had paranoid schizophrenia and could not have harbored malice-of-forethought at the time of the murder. In contrast, the prosecution-appointed psychiatrist held that Poddar was only schizoid, and that his mental state would make a charge of first- or second-degree murder appropriate. The Superior Court of Alameda County, California, convicted Poddar of second-degree murder. The verdict, however, was reversed because the judge erred in his instructions to the jury. Poddar was released and returned to India. The last information on Poddar was a letter in which he stated that he was happily married (Stone, 1976).

While the state was pursuing the criminal case, Tanya's parents initiated a wrongful-death suit against the Regents of the University of California, the psychologist and psychiatrists, and the police officers who were involved in the treatment of Poddar and the abortive attempt to commit him. The suit fueled a national debate concerning the limits of confidentiality with life-endangering patients.

The civil *Tarasoff* case was determined twice. In 1974 the California Supreme Court activated a duty to warn. The first decision led to so much controversy that, in an unusual move, the California Supreme court agreed to re-review the case. In the second decision in 1976, the court modified its reasoning in reaching its decision. After the second decision was issued, the first decision lost any binding authority even in California. All subsequent references to the *Tarasoff* decision refer to the second decision.

Tatiana Tarasoff's parents brought suit against the University of California and its employees on two major grounds: the failure to commit Poddar and the failure to warn Tanya of her peril. The defendants countered both charges. They argued that the California statutes protected them from liability for the failure to commit. Also, they argued that they should not have had to warn Tarasoff because predictions of dangerousness are too difficult to make with reasonable accuracy, and such warnings would have violated the confidentiality necessary for an effective psychotherapeutic relationship.

The court did not hold the defendants liable for failure to commit Poddar. They cited the relevant California statute that exempts public employees from liabilities for injuries resulting from decisions to release mental patients.

The court did, however, assess liability for the failure to warn Tarasoff of the danger to her. The decision was based, to a large extent, on the affirmative duty to act which arises out of the "special relationship" between a psychotherapist and a patient. According to the common law, an individual usually has no duty to control the behavior of another in order to protect a third party. Nevertheless, once a "special relationship" has been established, the law may require affirmative obligations. These socially recognized relationships, such as parent to child or possessor of land to renter, imply a legal duty to attempt to protect others from harm, or to warn them of potential harm. For example, parents must secure the protection of their children, and physicians are required to protect the public by reporting the existence of a contagious disease. In most states at the time of the *Tarasoff* decision, physicians and other health professionals were required to report suspected child abuse or neglect.

Furthermore, custodians of patients in psychiatric or similar institutions have a duty to protect or warn third persons about dangerous patients. In several court cases (e.g., *Fair v. United States*, 1956; *Underwood v. United States*, 1966) hospitals, or doctors in their employ, were found liable for failure to warn murder victims of the dangerousness of released mental patients.

In this regard, *Tarasoff* provided nothing new in the area of tort liability. The court merely applied inpatient tort law to an outpatient setting.

The court acknowledged some validity in the defendants' argument that dangerousness is hard to predict, but they ruled that difficulty in determining dangerousness does not remove the obligation of psychotherapists to protect others when such a determination is made. The court also rejected the contention that the provisions of the Landerman-Petris-Short Act prevented the defendants from disclosing information to the intended victim. The Landerman-Petris-Short Act delineates several exceptions to confidentiality, but it does not include warning potential victims as an exception to confidentiality. The court, however, held that the Act only covers information acquired in the involuntary commitment of patients or acquired by employees at state and county hospitals. Other mental health professionals do not fall under the provisions of the Act.

The court also recognized that psychotherapy requires confidentiality to be effective. Justice Tobriner, writing for the majority opinion, stated, however:

> Public policy favoring protection of the confidential character of the patient-psychotherapist communications must yield to the extent to which disclosure is essential to avert danger to others since the protective privilege ends when the public peril begins. (pp. 334-337)

Because the *Tarasoff* decision has been subject to so many misinterpretations, it is important to know what the *Tarasoff* court did not say. The court did not require psychotherapists to issue a warning every time a patient talks about an urge or fantasy to harm someone. On the contrary, the court stated that "a therapist should not be encouraged routinely to reveal such threats . . . unless such disclosure is necessary to avert danger to others" (p. 347). The court did not require psychotherapists to interrogate their clients or to conduct independent investigations when the identity of the victim is unknown. Rather, the duty to protect arises only when the victim has been identified or could be identified upon "a moment's reflection" (p. 345, fn 11). Finally, the court did not specify that warning the intended victim was the only required response when danger arises. On the contrary, the court stated that the "discharge of such duty may require the therapist to take one or more of various steps, depending on the nature of the case, including warning the intended victim" (p. 334). The therapist may initiate an involuntary commitment, notify the police, modify the treatment, or take other steps to deter the violence.

DISSENTING OPINIONS

The *Tarasoff* decision was not unanimous and included a strong dissent by Justice Clark. Clark disagreed with the interpretation given to the application of the confidentiality sections of the Landerman-Petris-Short Act. He believed that this Act did apply to the mental health professionals involved, and that it prevented them from disclosing information. In addition to the alleged statutory misinterpretation found in the majority decision, Justice Clark stated that the decision was also poor public policy. "While offering virtually no benefit to society, such a duty will frustrate psychiatric treatment, invade fundamental patient rights and increase violence" (p. 358).

Justice Mosk also wrote a separate opinion in which he agreed in part and disagreed in part with the majority decision. Justice Mosk concurred in the result in this case because the "defendant therapists did in fact predict that Poddar would kill and were therefore negligent in failing to warn of that danger" (p. 353). The major point in his dissent concerned the standards the court used to judge the failure to predict a patient's violence. The majority held that the psychotherapists were required to adhere to the "standards of the profession" in predicting danger. Mosk asked, "What standards?" He noted that psychotherapists have no unique ability to predict danger and have been "incredibly inaccurate" in their predictions. Instead of adhering to the standards of the profession, Mosk wrote:

> I would restructure the rule designed by the majority to eliminate all reference to conformity to standards of the profession in predicting violence. If a psychiatrist does in fact predict violence, then a duty to warn arises. (p. 354)

BACKGROUND ON DUTY TO PROTECT

Many psychotherapists resented the "new" legal intrusions into clinical practice. However, a study of the background of American common law shows that the "duty to protect" (*Tarasoff* doctrine) is not new. Rather, it is part of a legal tradition that has developed over many years. The only thing unique about *Tarasoff* is that it applied old legal principles regarding tort liability and negligence to a new context (Beigler, 1984).

Anglo-American law distinguishes between injuries arising out of an action ("misfeasance") and injuries arising out of nonaction ("nonfeasance"). According to traditional law, parties could be held responsible for injuries arising out of misfeasance, that is, injuries caused by their actions. They could not, however, be held responsible for injuries arising out of nonfeasance (Kamenar, 1984).

According to this distinction, no person is required to come to the aid of another. Consequently, expert swimmers may sit on the dock and watch a person drown; physicians are not required to respond to the call of one who is dying; travelers are not obligated to stop at the scene of a traffic accident to assist the victims; and members of the public are not required to donate vital organs for a life-saving transplant or to give blood for a life-saving transfusion. Such decisions are only subject to the personal consciences of the individuals involved.

The general rule of providing no legal remedies for nonfeasance gradually eroded for those in "public callings." The first such public calling referred to innkeepers who had an affirmative duty to protect their guests, or public carriers who had a duty to protect their passengers. An innkeeper could not passively permit dangerous conditions to exist in the guest's room without warning the guest beforehand or removing the threat. Similarly, a public carrier had to take reasonable steps to insure that passengers were safely transported. The rule for nonfeasance was later expanded to include any situation where a "special relationship" existed.

Paragraph 315 of the *Restatement of Torts* expresses this rule:

> There is no duty to control the conduct of a third person as to prevent him from causing physical harm to another unless: (a) a special relation exists between the actor and the third person which imposes a duty upon the actor to control the third person's conduct. (American Law Institute, 1966, p. 857)

The key phrase is "special relation." Courts have held that a special relationship exists when a person voluntarily agrees to assume responsibility for another person. Consequently, jailers are responsible for the conduct of their prisoners, parents for the conduct of their children, and professionals who run mental hospitals are responsible for the behavior of the patients. The responsibility here is not absolute. Rather, the custodians are expected to use reasonable care. There is no liability when the custodians use reasonable care, or when the custodians do not know, nor have any reason to know, that more precautions are needed.

The definition of the special relationship is one of the major features of the *Tarasoff* debate. The concept of special relationship has been applied to physicians and hospitals in a number of contexts. Psychiatric hospitals have a duty to use reasonable care when they release psychiatric patients into the community and to prevent the escape of dangerous patients (see, e.g., *Fair v. United States*, 1956; *Underwood v. United States*, 1966). In addition, physicians have a responsibility to warn patients if their medications could interfere with their ability to operate machinery or drive an automobile (*Kaiser v. Suburban Transportation System*, 1965). Doctors are liable if they negligently fail to diagnose contagious diseases (*Hofmann v. Blackmon*, 1970), or if they diagnose the disease but negligently fail to warn members of the patient's family (*Skillings v. Allen*, 1919; *Wojcik v. Aluminum Company of America*, 1959).

According to the *Tarasoff* decision, Dr. Moore, the psychotherapist, had a "special relationship" with Prosenjit Poddar. This special relationship created the obligation to act to protect an identifiable victim from Poddar's predicted behavior.

LIVING WITH TARASOFF

The *Tarasoff* decision created anger and confusion among mental health professionals. Some of the confusion was due to a misunderstanding or misinterpretation of the court's decision. Some of the anger and confusion, however, was a reasonable reaction to an apparent legal intrusion into clinical practice that created more questions than it answered. No statutory law or court decision can predict all the circumstances that will apply in future cases. The *Tarasoff* decision, however, seemed to leave too many questions unanswered. For example, the decision did not give much guidance on what would constitute appropriate steps to discharge the duty to protect. Nor did it delineate where psychotherapists can find the "standards of their profession" in determining when the duty to protect arises. Furthermore, the *Tarasoff* case was binding only in California, and practitioners in other states could not predict whether courts in their states would follow *Tarasoff* reasoning.

Tarasoff is only one of many decisions regarding the liability of psychotherapists who are treating dangerous patients. Like similar cases, it raises questions of how to balance the safety of the community with the privacy of the patient. It also raises questions of social utility: Does this rule, as Justice Clark stated, vitiate the effectiveness of psychotherapy and increase the danger to society?

While legal scholars and researchers debate these issues, mental health professionals must make daily decisions concerning the treatment of their potentially dangerous patients. Fortunately, psychotherapists need not treat their patients in a legal vacuum. Subsequent case law has clarified some of the questions that *Tarasoff* raised. Clinical research and experience provide guidelines for dealing with dangerous patients which fulfill legal responsibilities as well as obligations to patients and community. We cannot answer all questions, but we can narrow their scope considerably. Although the *Tarasoff* decision has problems and shortcomings, it is a decision with which therapists can live. Furthermore, it may, with minor modifications, be considered a good decision.

SUBSEQUENT CALIFORNIA CASES

Subsequent California cases have amplified the *Tarasoff* rules. These cases have addressed the issues of threats to unidentified persons, the assessment of dangerousness when the patient has not made a direct verbal threat, and the duty to protect persons who have a "close relationship" to the identified victim.

Mavroudis v. Superior Court for County of San Mateo (1980) dealt with the issue of threats to unspecified persons. In this case, a hospital released a boy into the custody of his parents, whom he subsequently assaulted with a hammer. The parents requested access to their son's psychiatric records to determine if the hospital knew that they were identifiable victims of their son. The *Mavroudis* court reaffirmed the middle ground initially given in a footnote in *Tarasoff* (p. 345, fn 11). It stated that even if the patient did not specifically identify an intended victim, the psychotherapist could often determine the victim's identity through a "moment's reflection." Yet, on the other hand, the *Mavroudis* court recognized that the psychotherapists need not interrogate the patient or conduct a special investigation to learn the identity of the intended victim.

Another case dealt with vague and global threats against unspecified persons. In *Thompson v. County of Alameda* (1980), a juvenile had made threats to kill someone if he were released. Nevertheless, the county released the juvenile into the custody of his mother without discussing his threats with her or anyone else. Within 24 hours of his release, he sexually assaulted and murdered a neighborhood child. The court ruled that the juvenile-justice authorities were immune from liability and had no obligation to warn the community, the police, or his mother. The court stated that giving a general warning for nonspecific threats made by each person released would be unwieldy, of little practical benefit, and would undermine the rehabilitative purposes of probation.

The *Thompson* case, however, included a strong dissent which said that warning an intended victim was not the only possible action the defendants could have taken. It was argued that the defendants had a duty to take reasonable steps to prevent the harm because the violence was foreseeable. The dissenters said that, under the circumstances of this case, the juvenile-justice authorities should have notified the boy's mother of the threats.

The assessment of dangerousness does not necessarily require a verbal threat (*Jablonski v. United States*, 1983). Jablonski murdered his live-in girlfriend, Melinda Kimball. Prior to the murder, Jablonski had attempted to rape Kimball's mother. The mother reported this event to the police, who referred Jablonski to a Veterans' Administration hospital and warned a VA psychiatrist about his potential violence. The psychiatrist failed to record or pass on this warning.

Jablonski refused to stay in the hospital, but he did attend several outpatient sessions, accompanied by Kimball. She told several psychotherapists that she was afraid of Jablonski and each of them advised her to leave him. She followed their advice and left him, but Jablonski murdered her when she returned to their apartment.

The court found the psychiatrists negligent for failure to record and pass along the warning from the police, for failure to secure prior records, and for failure to warn the victim. While the psychiatrists had advised Kimball to move away from Jablonski, the court concluded: "The warnings . . . were totally unspecific and inadequate under the circumstances" (p. 398). In addition, the court held that psychotherapists could be held liable even when they did not have actual knowledge of dangerousness because they "should have known."

The court followed a sound principle in this case; under certain circumstances, a reasonably prudent psychotherapist may predict dangerousness even without a specific verbal threat. In this case, however, the court did not appear to apply that principle appropriately. It seems unreasonable that the court found the psychiatrists' advice to Kimball to leave Jablonski to be "nonspecific and inadequate."

The duty to protect was extended in the case of *Hedlund v. Superior Court of Orange County* (1983). LaNita Wilson brought action against the psychotherapists, alleging that they failed to warn her that one of their patients, Stephen Wilson, was of imminent danger to her. LaNita and Stephen were lovers, but they were never married. (Their identical last name is a coincidence.) Stephen had told a psychotherapist of his intention to seriously harm LaNita. Subsequently, Stephen shot and wounded LaNita and emotionally traumatized her infant son, who was with her at the time of the shooting.

The court concluded that the defendants had actual knowledge of Stephen's dangerousness and should have warned LaNita. Furthermore, the court agreed that the duty to protect should have extended to the infant child. The court stated: "nor is it unreasonable to recognize the existence of a duty to persons in close relationship to the object of a patient's threat, for the therapist must consider the existence of such persons both in evaluating the seriousness of the danger posed by the patient and in determining the appropriate steps to be taken to protect the named victim" (p. 47).

The *Hedlund* case appears to extend *Tarasoff*. The other California cases merely amplify rules already stated in *Tarasoff*. The implications of the *Hedlund* decision are unclear. The decision does not provide guidance on how to identify who is in a "close relationship." Nor does it specify how psychotherapists should act to protect such persons. Consider the hypothetical case in which an elementary-school teacher is an identifiable victim of foreseeable danger. If warning the teacher is required, must the psychotherapist also warn the school children, since they are obvious bystanders? Or should other teachers or school officials be warned? The *Hedlund* case suggests that if a warning is warranted, the identified teacher should be alerted to the danger to both herself and to her pupils. The teacher may then decide how to proceed to protect those in close relationship to her.

APPLICATION OF *TARASOFF* IN OTHER STATES

Since the *Tarasoff* decision was issued in 1976, numerous courts in other states have dealt with the issues raised by the California cases. Courts have evaluated the relevance of the *Tarasoff* doctrine in a number of situations in addition to outpatient settings. The principles have been applied to the negligent release of patients from hospitals; the failure to supervise patients adequately within hospitals, thereby permitting them to escape; the failure to commit patients; and the failure to supervise patients who are conditionally released or who are under an outpatient commitment order.

This section will also evaluate the applications of *Tarasoff* to several clinical settings. Some of the factual details of each case are presented so that readers can better appreciate the kinds of actual situations that may arise. This case review is not intended to be comprehensive. Instead, the cases were selected because they represented common legal and clinical problems.

APPLICATION TO OUTPATIENT SETTINGS

The application of *Tarasoff* to outpatient as well as inpatient settings usually hinges on the factual circumstances dealing with the foreseeability of the danger and the presence of an identifiable victim. Several case examples that illustrate these principles are described.

In *McIntosh v. Milano* (1979), a New Jersey court accepted the *Tarasoff* doctrine. In this case, a New Jersey psychiatrist had been treating a patient, Lee Morganstein, for 2 years before Morganstein murdered his next-door neighbor, Ms. McIntosh. Morganstein apparently felt angry with McIntosh because she did not reciprocate his romantic interest. He had reportedly fired a BB gun at her house and car sometime previous to the murder, but Dr. Milano testified that the patient had never expressed any feelings of violence toward her or made any threats to kill her. Although the therapist had failed to predict accurately, this failure was based on his professional judgment that the patient was not violent. The jury found no negligence.

Perhaps the most famous case of failure to warn in an outpatient setting is *Brady v. Hopper* (1983). In this case, John Hinckley's psychiatrist had failed to warn President Reagan of Hinckley's plan to assassinate him. In the assassination attempt, James

Brady, a presidential aide, and two Secret Service employees were seriously injured. The central issue in *Brady* was the rule that negligence requires foreseeable violence and an identifiable victim. The plaintiffs held that the possibility that Hinckley would act dangerously was foreseeable, and that the psychiatrist owed a duty to the public at large. The court disagreed, noting that the *Tarasoff* duty to protect was limited to identifiable victims. Instead, the court held that "unless [a] patient makes specific threats, [the] possibility that he may inflict injury on another is vague, speculative, and [a] matter of conjecture" (p. 1333).

In *Hasenei v. United States* (1982), an outpatient from a Veterans' Administration medical center had gotten drunk and driven his car recklessly, causing an accident and killing a pedestrian. The plaintiff claimed that the VA should have attempted to hospitalize the outpatient, alter his medication, or notify the Department of Motor Vehicles that he was incapable of driving safely. The court refused to find the VA liable. It noted that the civil commitment standards in Pennsylvania were very high and that the patient did not qualify under those standards. In addition, the court noted that the psychiatrist had no basis to predict that the patient would drive recklessly, let alone get involved in the accident with the specific victim. In other words, the accident was not foreseeable nor was the victim identifiable.

A different outcome occurred in *Peck v. The Counseling Service of Addison County* (1985). Here an outpatient told his counselor at a mental health clinic that he might burn down his parents' barn as an act of revenge against his father. In the session, however, the patient was dissuaded from such a course and promised not to carry out his threat. The counselor believed the patient and did not disclose the threats to any other staff members or to the patient's parents. Nevertheless, the patient burned the barn the next night.

The court found the counselor and her agency negligent. In this case, the patient had identified a "victim," but the question centered around whether the threats were serious and whether property damage fell within the purview of a duty to protect. Relying on expert witnesses, the court concluded that the background of the patient, which included a history of past assaultive behavior and alcohol abuse, made it foreseeable that he might be dangerous.

The court concluded that the counseling service was negligent for an inadequate record-keeping system, and that the counselor was negligent for failure to obtain prior records, failure to take a comprehensive history of the patient's reported brain damage and psychiatric status, and failure to consult her supervisor or any other therapists. One justice, however, disagreed with the majority and held that the counselor "in good faith did not believe there was any threat to person or property by the patient, and so no duty arises" (p. 428). Also notable is the extension of the duty to a counselor who was neither a psychologist nor a psychiatrist.

NEGLIGENT RELEASE OF PATIENTS

As noted earlier, the *Tarasoff* precedent was based, in part, on case law dealing with the negligent release of patients from psychiatric hospitals. The case law on negligent release has changed little since *Tarasoff*. Hospitals are liable for releasing or for granting leaves to dangerous patients when the decisions are made with negligence. In addition, hospitals are liable for negligently failing to prevent the escape of involuntarily committed, dangerous patients. The several cases discussed below illustrate the application of these principles.

In *Bradley Center v. Wessner* (1982), a man had admitted himself voluntarily to Bradley Center for depression and anger toward his wife for having an affair with another man. The woman had made known her intent to divorce her husband. During the weekend of February 7 and 8, 1975, Wessner had been given a pass to visit his children. During that time he secured a gun, confronted his wife and her paramour, and shot them both. The court held that the "criminal act was reasonably foreseeable . . . and that the death of their mother [Mrs. Wessner] was proximately caused by appellant's negligence" (p. 719). The crucial piece of evidence in this case was the nurse's notes of February 5th and 6th which recorded Mr. Wessner's threats against his wife. "He made a statement that he had a weapon and was just waiting for the right circumstances" (p. 719). Although the wife knew of the threats, the facility had the power to refuse the leave request because state law allowed it to detain voluntary patients for 48 hours before a release was mandated.

Tarasoff principles were applied in *Davis v. Lhim* (1983), where a psychiatrist released his patient, John Patterson, to the custody of his mother. Although the court report does not give a diagnosis for Patterson, it does note that he reported hallucinations, delusions of persecution, drug dependence, and alcoholism.

Two months after his release, Patterson became agitated and began firing a shotgun at the house of his aunt, where his mother was staying. His mother tried to talk Patterson out of shooting again, and then attempted to restrain him. In the struggle Patterson fired several more shots, one of which killed his mother.

Relying upon expert witnesses, the court held that the treating psychiatrists should have known that Patterson was dangerous and that his mother was an identifiable victim. The court made reference to a psychiatric note made in an emergency unit 2 years before the incident, which stated "he paces the floor and acts strangely, and keeps threatening his mother for money" (p. 490). On the basis of this note, the jury concluded that his mother was a foreseeable victim. It is interesting to note that Patterson did not kill his mother for money, but killed her accidentally while in a general rage. The court held that the hospital failed to use adequate judgment in releasing Patterson and owed a duty to his slain mother.

Unlike most other court decisions, this one may have applied *Tarasoff* inaccurately. Although it is impossible to evaluate a case fully on the basis of summaries found in the court opinions, it is doubtful that justice was served in this case. The duty to protect was evoked for a patient with no past history of violence on the basis of a 2-year-old case note alluding to threats against his mother for money. Furthermore, the 2-month interval between the release and the subsequent murder makes it appear that Patterson was not an imminent threat to his mother at the time of being released.

A federal court, however, showed more deference to psychotherapeutic judgment in the case of *White v. United States* (1986). Here a court-committed patient who was described as an "explosive personality" with low frustration tolerance had revealed fantasies of harming his wife with a gun. Later, the patient left the hospital grounds in violation of a court order and stabbed his wife 55 times with a pair of scissors. The court did not hold the psychotherapist liable for failure to warn the wife of her husband's fantasies because the "assessment was a reasonable one under the standards of her profession" (p. 102). The patient had no background of assaulting women and had no history of assaults at all in the past year. Furthermore, the patient had acknowledged that these thoughts were fantasies. The court did, however, find the hospital negligent for failure to prevent the patient from leaving the hospital grounds.

Several courts have refused to apply the *Tarasoff* decision when there was no foreseeable victim. For example, in *Doyle v. United States* (1982), an Army psychiatrist had evaluated and treated a 19-year-old man when he was having trouble adjusting to Army life. This man stated that "he joined the Army to learn to kill and indicated that he would use the knowledge to kill his parents" (p. 1280). The psychiatrist ordered an inpatient stay to evaluate the patient. During that stay the patient was placed on medication which rendered him cooperative and well-adjusted to the ward.

The Army psychiatrist concluded that "Carson verbalized his aggressive fantasies in order to shock people and compensate for a very inadequate personality" (p. 1281). He believed that "Carson's violent statements were manipulative attempts to make himself appear undesirable [for Army life]" (p. 1282). After his discharge from the Army, Carson killed a security guard on a college campus in an attempt to obtain weapons. The suit against the Army psychiatrist failed because the danger to the security guard was not reasonably foreseeable.

Similarly, hospitals are not liable if the danger is not foreseeable. In *Ross v. Central Louisiana State Hospital* (1980), a woman with a diagnosis of schizophrenia shot and killed her daughter and shot and injured her son 7 months after being discharged from a mental hospital. Her husband (the father of her two children) sued the hospital for failing to warn him that his wife would become violent if she did not take her medication. The treating psychiatrists testified that at the time of her release, the patient "had never exhibited any propensity toward violence nor could they have recommended her commitment since they did not consider her dangerous to herself or others" (p. 699). The court rejected the suit, noting that "a hospital cannot be expected to warn third persons of possible dangers which it could not foresee" (p. 700).

A few courts have expanded the *Tarasoff* rule so that psychotherapists are liable for harm caused by foreseeable danger even in the absence of specific foreseeable victims. For example, in *Lipari v. Sears* (1980), a psychiatric hospital was sued after its patient purchased a shotgun and randomly shot several people in a crowded nightclub. The federal court found a duty to protect even if the victim is not identifiable. In this specific case, however, the court did not rule on the merits of whether the psychotherapists were negligent in releasing the murderer, and the case was settled out of court.

COURT-ORDERED RELEASES

Psychotherapists and hospitals are not liable for court-ordered patient releases. In *Teasley v. United States* (1980), a woman was attacked by a former mental patient. The victim sued the hospital for releasing the patient. The suit failed because the hospital staff had requested an involuntary commitment of the patient but the court had rejected the request. This case differs substantially from *Hicks v. United States* (1975), where a plaintiff successfully sued hospital employees even though the patient was released by the court. In *Hicks*, the hospital staff had negligently failed to provide the court with full and accurate details of the patient's mental condition. In *Teasley*, the hospital staff correctly informed the court of the patient's dangerous qualities and told the court that he would be a danger to society if released.

FAILURE TO CONTROL OR COMMIT

Even before the *Tarasoff* decision, psychotherapists had been sued for a failure to commit their patients. These suits were based on the theory of professional negligence: that the psychotherapist had failed to use reasonable standards of treatment by failing to commit a patient. The last few years, however, have seen a shift in the common reasons for seeking liability or damages. It has become clear that most courts will not expand *Tarasoff* beyond its original limits. Consequently, plaintiffs have begun to seek damages on the premise of a duty to commit or control the patient.

FAILURE TO COMMIT BEFORE TARASOFF

Psychotherapists will not likely be held liable for failure to commit if the potential harm is not foreseeable. In *Paradies v. Benedictine Hospital* (1980), a voluntary patient left the hospital against medical advice and killed himself 3 weeks later. Although *Paradies* was decided 4 years after *Tarasoff*, the court did not rely on the *Tarasoff* precedent in reaching its decision. The court ruled that the hospital was not negligent for failing to commit the man because it lacked statutory ground to warrant a commitment. Even if mental health professionals have the statutory power to seek a commitment, they are not liable as long as they follow acceptable procedures in treating patients.

18

In *Fernandez v. Baruch* (1968), a physician had evaluated a patient for homicidal tendencies and had initiated treatment. He also recommended an involuntary commitment to a state hospital, but did not follow through with the commitment when the family protested. Subsequently, the man was returned to jail, where he hanged himself. The physician was not liable for the suicide because the act was not foreseeable.

Courts may, however, find liability when psychotherapists fail to initiate or further commitments when they are indicated. In *Greenberg v. Barbour* (1971), a physician had referred a patient for a civil commitment but failed to mention the life-endangering qualities of his behavior. The patient was not committed and subsequently assaulted a third party. The court held that the accepted standards of treatment involved conveying the life-endangering facts concerning the patient when seeking a commitment.

FAILURE TO COMMIT AFTER TARASOFF

As noted previously, the *Tarasoff* decision does not necessarily require psychotherapists to issue a warning when they believe that acts of violence are imminent. Those circumstances which give rise to a warning are often sufficient to impose a duty to seek involuntary hospitalization. The viability of the commitment option depends, in part, on the wording of the state's involuntary-commitment law.

State laws usually specify that the person must be severely mentally ill. In addition, the state law may require that the patient present a danger to self or others. Numerous states require an overt act before the patient fits the statutory definition of dangerousness. Other clinical data such as violent thoughts, fantasies, or verbal threats may not be sufficient, from a legal point of view, to justify a commitment.

Nevertheless, a psychotherapist could be held liable for failing to commit when commitment is justified and a tragedy occurs. The standard malpractice criteria will apply to psychotherapists who fail to commit in those circumstances. For malpractice principles to apply, the therapist must have a professional relationship with the patient, the therapist's treatment must fall below an acceptable standard of care, the patient must have been harmed, and the harm must have been caused by the therapist's inadequate or inappropriate treatment.

The three cases below illustrate how courts have applied the *Tarasoff* duty-to-control principles in specific cases. In the first case, *Currie v. United States* (1986), a district court gave specific guidelines for determining when the psychotherapist would be liable, but a federal appeals court later concluded that a state law provided immunity for hospitals and their staff. The second case, *Clark v. State* (1984), is an example of a court that did find the psychotherapists liable for a failure to commit. Finally, in *Abernathy v. United States* (1985), liability was not found primarily because the patient did not meet the statutory requirements for an involuntary civil commitment.

The most notable post-*Tarasoff* commitment case is *Currie v. United States* (1987). Here the psychotherapist had been treating a dangerous outpatient suffering from Post-Traumatic Stress Disorder. The patient had threatened to kill unspecified co-workers; the psychotherapists had sought professional consultation, encouraged the patient to hospitalize himself (the patient agreed but never fulfilled his promise), and issued a warning to the company and to the police. A commitment was not attempted, however, because the psychotherapists incorrectly concluded that the patient would not qualify under North Carolina's commitment law.

Although the patient later killed a co-worker in a shooting spree, the psychotherapists were exonerated from liability because the court was convinced that they had shown good faith in their actions. The district court claimed, however, that initiating a commitment could rise to the level of a "duty" when the patient poses a potentially life-endangering risk and qualifies for a commitment, even if a specific victim is not identified. "Arguably," the court said, "the patient who will kill wildly (rather than specifically identifiable victims) is the one *most* in need of confinement" (p. 1079).

A federal appeals court (*Currie v. United States*, 1987) in North Carolina disagreed that psychotherapists have a duty to commit. The appeals court cited a 1986 North Carolina statute that extended immunity from liability to federal hospitals and their staff (the VA psychiatrists were federal employees). Furthermore, the court concluded that imposing such a duty to commit would require psychotherapists to breach confidentiality, thereby undermining the therapist-patient relationship.

In *Clark v. State* (1984), a New York court found an outpatient mental health center negligent in failing to commit a patient with a long history of mental illness and suicidal tendencies. The patient had assaulted a woman with a knife, and the court upheld the victim's suit against the psychotherapist for the failure to commit his patient. The patient had a diagnosis of paranoid schizophrenia and a past record of assaultiveness. In early 1978, he began to deteriorate, probably due to a failure to take prescribed medication, or because of mixing the medication with street drugs.

The treatment records indicated that he was more likely to be a harm to himself than to others. Two of his friends had called the doctor to warn of his deteriorating mental state. The psychiatrist noted that the patient had not had a single episode of violence in 15 months and had become more cooperative with treatment; for instance, he had agreed to a short-term voluntary hospitalization several months before. Although he failed to attend his appointment with the psychiatrist the day before the assault, a psychiatric nurse had spoken to him on the phone 6 days before the assault, and that conversation "yielded nothing that would cause her to alert her doctor that . . . [he] was approaching a crisis" (p. 173). Despite this evidence, the court concluded by a three-to-two verdict that "this record and the testimony . . . indicate an almost casual consideration of the problems of a deeply troubled patient" (p. 172).

In hindsight, the psychiatrist had made an error in treating the patient, but his behavior was not as obviously negligent as the court concluded. The point of this case is that psychotherapists need to take great care when a client is in crisis. The failure to make one phone call or to follow up on a missed appointment could mean the difference between the perception of acceptable and negligent treatment.

In *Abernathy v. United States* (1985), a Sioux Indian was convicted of murder when he assaulted a clothing-store clerk with a bat. The attendant had caught the man trying to steal a pair of blue jeans. The attendant's family sued the Bureau of Indian Affairs and the Indian Health Service, claiming that they should have committed the assailant for a previous assault. The allegation, however, was rejected. The court noted that, although the assailant had epilepsy, he would not have qualified for a commitment because he did not have the severe degree of mental disability required under the Crow Creek Tribal Code for civil commitments. Furthermore, a neurologist testified that the assailant "had the ability to control his behavior and his violent temper was a learned behavior pattern" (p. 190, fn 4).

OUTPATIENT COMMITMENT

The practice of outpatient commitment has become more common in recent years. An outpatient commitment permits the patient to reside in the community contingent on receiving continuing mental health treatment. The case cited below illustrates the application of tort law to outpatient commitments. We expect the frequency of these cases to increase as outpatient commitments become more frequent.

In *Cain v. Rijken* (1986), the Oregon Supreme Court refused to grant a summary judgment in a trial for failure to commit. Instead, the court ruled that the case must go to trial to determine if the facts warranted a verdict against the defendants. This case was significant because it dealt with the responsibility of mental health professionals in dealing with persons who are under a conditional release or an outpatient commitment. In this case, a former psychiatric patient had been released from the hospital on the condition that he attend a psychiatric day-treatment program. Around New Year's Day, he began to deteriorate mentally and to experience hallucinations. He missed a therapy appointment on January 2, 1981, and on January 4, he drove his car at 70 mph in a 35 mph zone, ran through two traffic lights, and collided with another car, killing the driver.

The court held that the day-treatment program had a duty to monitor the patient and report any substantial deterioration in his behavior or mental status to the Psychiatric Services Review Board. Although the Board could not have controlled him, as in an inpatient setting, they could have requested a recommitment. The court did not decide on the merits of this case, but held that the issues involved were disputable questions of fact to be resolved by a lower court. It seems likely that sponsors of outpatient commitments will be expected to provide closer supervision of their patients than would be true for noncommitted outpatients.

IMMUNITY LAWS

Generally, government officials who create statutes and regulations, and administrators of facilities who must exercise their judgment in implementing the regulations, are immune from liability. However, psychotherapists and others who actually provide the hands-on patient care are liable for failure to exercise due care. Courts often make the distinction about which officials are immune from liability by examining whether the actions or judgments were "discretionary" or "ministerial."

Discretionary functions refer to judgment calls about how to implement regulations. Examples would be decisions as to whether regulations permit the institution to grant a leave from a hospital for a patient to visit family or friends, or whether an open-door policy for suicidal patients is an acceptable treatment approach. Ministerial functions, in contrast, refer to specific actions taken with specific patients by psychotherapists or other personnel who are in direct contact with the patient. With this distinction, a hospital administrator may be held immune from liability for implementing treatment programs permitted by state law, but in the same case a psychotherapist could be found liable for negligence in carrying out the treatment plan.

Immunity laws provide a patchwork of exceptions that vary considerably among the states. The wording of immunity laws is important in determining the scope of possible liability. For example, in *Sharpe v. South Carolina Department of Mental Health* (1984), a court held that the hospital superintendent and physicians were immune from liability for the release of a patient who eventually shot and killed a person. However, the court concluded that the officials were liable for their treatment of the patient and for failure to notify the public of his discharge. Although the physicians were statutorily immune for part of their conduct, they were not completely immune from lawsuits.

Other immunity statutes provide protection only for decisions made in good faith. Unreasonable acts or releases made in bad faith would not qualify under such a statute (e.g., *Leverett v. State*, 1978). Sometimes the immunity only applies to the government and not to employees (e.g., *Davis v. Lhim*, 1983).

The doctrine of sovereign immunity was very loosely applied in *Sherrill v. Wilson* (1983). In this case, a mother filed suit against four physicians employed by the state of Missouri for the wrongful death of her son who had been murdered by a patient who had been committed to the St. Joseph State Hospital. After 2 days, the psychiatrists gave the patient a pass to leave the hospital. He did not return from the pass, and the hospital did not notify the police to have him returned to custody. Shortly after he left the hospital, the patient shot and killed a man. The court held that the treating physicians did not owe a duty to protect the public at large, and that the decision to grant a pass was within their judgment.

LIABILITY FOR SUICIDES

Recent large-scale epidemiological studies have shown that the rate of suicide has increased substantially over the last 50 years. Young persons in the United States have a rate of suicide which is 10 times higher than that of their grandparents. Suicide is one of the leading causes of death among American teenagers. Not only is depression much more common, but major depression episodes are occurring earlier for young Americans (Seligman, 1989).

Few situations can upset a psychotherapist as much as a patient's suicide. It is bound to jar the confidence of even the most competent psychotherapist. He or she may spend many hours trying to second-guess the treatment plan, wondering what could have been done differently. The reactions of the family members may vary considerably. Some relatives readily acknowledge the efforts of psychotherapists and thank them for their efforts. Others may display extreme and irrational hostility. In addition to personal anguish, the psychotherapist may face legal problems. Patient suicides are one of the most frequent causes of malpractice suits.

Knapp and VandeCreek (1983) have reviewed several criteria for assessing professional liability in cases of suicide. Generally, courts will not find therapists liable when the suicide attempt was not foreseeable. Therefore, no liability has been found when cooperative and apparently contented patients suddenly attempted suicide (*Carlino v. State*, 1968; *Dalton v. State*, 1970), or when an aggressive patient failed to reveal suicidal intent (*Paradies v. Benedictine Hospital*, 1980). In contrast, courts have held practitioners or hospitals culpable when the treatment plan overlooked or neglected evidence of suicidal tendencies (*Dinnerstein v. United States*, 1973).

In evaluating liability, courts also usually assess the reasonableness of professional judgment in the treatment of a suicidal patient. The failure to take reasonable precautions when suicidal intent is obvious would be grounds for liability. Nevertheless, courts have been generous in deciding what precautions are acceptable. Practitioners must only demonstrate that reasonable precautions were taken. As described below, the acceptable forms of treatment have become more varied in recent years.

Finally, courts will evaluate the thoroughness with which the treatment plan was implemented. Thus, in *Comiskey v. State of*

New York (1979), a hospital (but not the physician) was found liable for failure to implement the physician's instructions to observe closely a suicidal patient. In contrast, the failure of a therapist to inform other staff members about the suicidal potential of a patient would leave the therapist at fault but absolve the uninformed staff (Perr, 1985).

INPATIENT SUICIDES

Plaintiffs can present legal actions for inpatient suicides against the hospital and/or the psychotherapists. The plaintiffs generally will make the malpractice suit against the physicians or psychotherapists within the hospital if they have staff or hospital privileges. Although these professionals may use the hospital facilities, they are assumed to be independent and responsible for their professional judgments.

In some situations, however, the plaintiff could also sue the hospital. The hospital could be liable if it negligently hired or trained its employees, supervised them inadequately, or tolerated hazardous facilities. In addition, if the hospital employed the physicians or psychotherapists, then the hospital could be sued for the negligent actions of the staff members under the doctrine of vicarious liability. The negligent employees, however, may not be entirely free from liability because the hospital could, in turn, sue them for the financial loss incurred by their actions (King, 1977).

In considering malpractice actions for inpatient suicides, the courts have slowly but steadily changed the standards of liability from an earlier "custodial model" to a more recent "open-door" model. According to the custodial model, patients were hospitalized to diagnose suicidal intent and then to protect them from their self-destructive impulses through close supervision. The strict standard of supervision turned psychotherapists into jailers with white coats.

Mary McCarthy described the strict custodial model in her novel, *The Group* (1964). Kay was committed involuntarily to Payne Whitney Clinic by her husband. One day, when she received a visit from her friend Polly, Kay exclaimed:

> "Heavens, I'm glad you're here! You don't know the terrible things they've been doing to me, Polly." Last night the nurses had taken her belt away from her. "I can't wear my dress without a belt." They had taken her

nightgown sash too ("Look!") and they tried to take her wedding ring, but she would not let them. "We had a frightful struggle, practically a wrestling match, but then the head nurse came and said to let me keep it for the night. . . . After that, they made me open my mouth and looked in to see if I had any removable bridges. . . ." "I gather," Kay went on in a different tone, "that they think I want to commit suicide. They keep peering at me through those slats in the door. Did they expect me to hang myself with my belt? And what was I supposed to do with my wedding ring? Swallow it." Polly's answer was prompt; she thought the nurses would have done better to explain it to Kay. (pp. 325-326)

Kay's experiences illustrate the shortcomings of the protective model. Although the suicidal precautions prevented Kay from attempting suicide, they also deprived her of basic sources of dignity and pleasure.

But even when the hospital applied the custodial model, there was no guarantee that patients could not commit suicide. Nonetheless, the courts have found liability only for reasonably foreseeable suicide attempts. In *Moore v. United States* (1963), the hospital was not found negligent when the patient pried open the detention screen from the third floor and jumped out. Although the patient had delusions and paranoid ideation, he had shown no evidence of suicidal intent. Similarly, in *Hirsch v. State* (1960), the hospital was absolved of blame when a patient committed suicide with capsules he had secreted. The hospital employees had stripped him naked and searched him. No one had reason to suspect that he had successfully concealed barbiturates.

The standards required by the courts in treating suicidal patients changed with the prevailing judgment of mental health experts. Courts would no longer require strict observation in all suicidal cases. This philosophy was expressed in *Dinnerstein v. United States* (1973): "[Not] every potential suicide must be locked in a padded cell. The law and modern psychiatry have now both come to the belated conclusion that an overly restrictive environment can be as destructive as a permissive one" (p. 38). Now the courts recognize that the psychotherapist must balance the benefits of treatment against the risks of freedom.

Psychotherapists must use reasonable professional judgment in assessing the therapeutic risks of freedom. They must carefully assess decisions to reduce the supervision of suicidal patients, whether these involve a transfer to a less restrictive ward or a leave or discharge out of the hospital. Of course, when the patient is dangerously suicidal, the hospital must still provide close supervision. "An open door policy does not mean an open window policy for highly suicidal patients" (Knapp & Vande-Creek, 1983, p. 277).

Inpatient units and their staff are on safer ground if they establish formal, written procedures for handling suicidal inpatients. Although the decision to place a patient on suicidal watch is usually made at the discretion of the treating physician, the exact procedures for the suicidal watch must conform to hospital policy. Hospital policies vary as to whether a psychiatric consultation is required, whether the observer should have certain qualifications, what furniture and personal items may be provided in the patient's room, frequency of review, and whether formal records of the observations are kept (Goldberg, 1987).

Perr (1985) described an example of the liability incurred when written policies are absent. A physician ordered observations of a suicidal patient, but the hospital had no written policy on what constituted observation of a patient. One nurse watched the patient constantly, but a second nurse checked the patient every 15 minutes. Apparently between the second nurse's observations, the patient hanged herself.

OUTPATIENT SUICIDES

The principles for establishing liability for outpatient suicides are generally the same as for inpatient cases. Psychotherapists must use reasonable standards of care in the diagnosis of suicidal intent and the development and implementation of a treatment plan. That is, psychotherapists should take seriously all suicidal gestures and threats. It is generally agreed that the potential for suicide increases if the patient has developed a specific plan and has the means to carry out a threat. Suicidal potential is also enhanced if the patient had made prior attempts or is experiencing protracted health problems. In assessing liability, courts have usually reviewed three criteria: foreseeability of the suicide attempt, reasonableness of professional judgment (e.g., severely depressed patients require more precautionary care than do less severely depressed patients), and thoroughness with which the treatment plan was implemented.

In *Runyon v. Reid* (1973), the family of a deceased patient sued a mental health foundation and a psychiatrist because the patient had taken a lethal dose of the sleeping pills that had been prescribed for him. The court found that the patient's suicidal intent was not foreseeable, and hence, it exonerated the clinic and the psychiatrist. Although this case involved a psychiatrist, it illustrates a principle which applies equally to nonmedical psychotherapists who treat outpatients: A psychotherapist using acceptable diagnostic and treatment procedures is not likely to be held liable for unforeseen suicide attempts.

Jails are an especially high-risk setting for suicides. Some new prisoners, under the stress of incarceration coupled with other preexisting problems, may be at high risk for suicide. While a jail is similar to a hospital in that both are tightly controlled institutional settings, the jail environment differs in being generally more destructive of self-esteem and confidence.

Knowledge of HIV infection substantially increases the risks of suicide. Marzuk et al. (1988) found that the relative risk of suicide in men (ages 20 to 59) with AIDS was 36 times the rate of men (ages 20 to 59) without AIDS and 66 times that of the general population. The high rate of suicide may be due to the psychological stress of having a painful and fatal disease, or it may be caused by AIDS dementia, or both. Psychotherapists may want to consider referring HIV/AIDS patients to support groups to supplement psychotherapy and other interventions.

There is no duty to warn relatives of potential suicide victims. In *Bellah v. Greenson* (1978), a California court refused to extend the duty to protect to suicidal patients. A psychiatrist was treating a young adult woman who subsequently committed suicide. Although she had revealed suicidal ideation to her psychiatrist, he had not warned her parents. Her parents brought suit, alleging that the psychiatrist had a responsibility to warn them of their daughter's suicidal tendencies. The court disagreed, stating that "*Tarasoff* requires only that a therapist disclose the contents of a confidential communication where the risk to be prevented thereby is the danger of violent assault, and not where the risk of harm is self-inflicted harm or property damage" (pp. 539-540). Although the therapist was not required to make a warning, California law permitted him to do so.

The *Bellah* ruling was narrow and dealt only with the duty to warn with suicidal patients. It did not allege generally negligent treatment. Of course, psychotherapists could be held liable for general negligence in treating suicidal patients.

The outpatient psychotherapist must determine the foreseeability of a suicide attempt according to acceptable professional standards. Unfortunately, a psychotherapist cannot predict the likelihood of a suicide attempt with as much precision as a physician can determine the presence of a broken bone. Instead, the decision rests upon a constellation of features, including the patient's report of intent to commit suicide, previous suicide attempts, the possibility of manipulativeness in the threats, amount of social support available to the patient, degree of depression, and the patient's cooperativeness. This list of features is not exhaustive, and psychotherapists may consider a myriad of clinical factors in making their treatment decisions.

The need for accurate documentation may be a shibboleth, but the experiences of lawyers and forensic psychotherapists show that accurate documentation of treatment and the patient's cooperation are extremely important (Soisson, VandeCreek, & Knapp, 1987). The psychotherapists can only prove that they provided adequate treatment through careful documentation. The lack of documentation may fatally cripple the defendants' case, even if the therapist had acted in a conscientious and professionally sound manner. Numerous case consultations have supported this conclusion, including a case where the consultant believed there was no negligence on the part of the treating staff, but "the almost complete lack of records left a legitimate issue as to the fact and so the settlement against the hospital and psychiatrist was made" (Perr, 1985, p. 217). The settlement in that case was for $500,000.

Documentation should be explicit about treatment decisions, such as to hospitalize or not to hospitalize the patient. In addition, the psychotherapists should carefully document any decision to reduce the frequency or intensity of observations of suicidal patients. Discharged patients should be given follow-up appointments, because suicide rates are especially high shortly after discharge.

Some of the precautions that outpatient therapists should take with suicidal patients are well-established. Attempts should be made to hospitalize or provide close monitoring of seriously suicidal persons, amounts of medication distributed should be nonlethal, psychotherapists should be available as needed on a 24-hour basis, and frequent therapeutic contacts must be offered. Deviations from these norms should be documented and justified.

An increase in the involvement of a support system for a suicidal patient may also be indicated, and significant others may have to be warned of the patient's suicidal potential. Involving the patient's family in treatment has several advantages. The support and sensitive watchfulness provided by the family can be a strong factor in promoting recovery. Also, should the patient actually commit suicide, the therapist already has established communication channels and, hopefully, a good relationship with the family. This may facilitate a healthy resolution of sorrow and grief; and given such a relationship, the family is less likely to initiate litigation against the therapist (Knapp & VandeCreek, 1983).

Often the psychotherapist must make a decision whether or not to seek an involuntary civil commitment for a seriously suicidal patient. The standard in judging this decision is that of traditional negligence. There is no liability *per se* for failure to commit a suicidal patient. Rather, the decision should be made on the basis of acceptable professional judgment.

For example, in *Bates v. Denney* (1990), a court ruled that a psychiatrist was not liable for the suicide of a 33-year-old man who had committed suicide the day after he was released from the hospital. The court noted that expert evidence supported the opinion of the treating psychiatrist that an involuntary commitment would have reduced the patient's receptivity to treatment. The expert testified that "during previous hospitalizations Mr. Bates exhibited resistant behavior to the ministrations of the staff" (p. 303). After previous hospitalizations, he had often missed outpatient appointments and quit taking medication.

REFUSALS TO EXPAND *TARASOFF* RULES

Plaintiffs have made various unsuccessful attempts to have the *Tarasoff* decision expanded. One court refused to find liability when the patient's husband withheld information about her violent behavior from the doctor. In *Matter of Estate of Votteler* (1982), Lola, a patient of Dr. Votteler, had seriously injured a woman by driving an automobile over her. Dr. Votteler had treated Lola for many years and hospitalized her twice. The injured woman sued Dr. Votteler because, she claimed, he should have warned his patient's husband about her violent nature and that the husband could have warned her. Lola had a background of violence, especially toward her husband. Although the doctor presumably knew something about her violent nature, her husband withheld a lot of information about her violent behavior from Dr. Votteler. At the trial the husband testified that he "did not tell the doctor about Lola's violence because he wasn't specifically asked about her behavior" (p. 761). The assaulted woman also knew about Lola's violent and threatening behavior but "she contends that she would have taken the situation seriously only if a warning originated with a professional like Dr. Votteler" (p. 761).

The court rejected the *Tarasoff* claim. The doctor was not required to issue a warning because the plaintiff already had more knowledge about the danger than the doctor.

Similarly, in *Wagshall v. Wagshall* (1989) the court failed to find the psychotherapists liable for the assault of a wife on her husband. The court noted that the husband and wife had terminated treatment several months before the assault occurred, that, as part of the treatment, they had agreed to place their firearms in a location which was not easily accessible, and that the wife had tried to shoot her husband just 5 weeks before she actually shot him.

Two courts refused to extend *Tarasoff* so that the psychiatrists could be liable to the assailants-patients. In *Cole v. Taylor* (1981), a former patient sued her psychiatrist on the grounds that he failed to prevent her from murdering her former husband. The plaintiff had received psychiatric treatment from the defendant psychiatrist for an unspecified mental disorder in May 1977. Several months later she shot and killed her former husband. She was charged, tried, and convicted of first-degree murder. Later she sued her psychiatrist on the ground that his treatment of her was negligent because he failed to stop her from murdering her ex-husband. She also invoked the *Tarasoff* decision, because, she claimed, the psychiatrist failed to warn her ex-husband of the danger to him.

Her claim was quickly rejected. The court stated that the *Tarasoff* decision was inapplicable because it only dealt with the duty to the intended victim and not to the assailant. Furthermore, the court noted that "as a general rule [a] person cannot maintain action if . . . he must rely in whole or in part, on [an] illegal or immoral act or transaction to which he is a party" (p. 766). The court did not elaborate on the social harm which would be done if murderers could act willfully and then project responsibility for their acts upon psychotherapists.

In *Veverka v. Cash* (1982), a former patient claimed that his psychiatrist failed to prevent him from torching an apartment building, which led to five deaths. The patient was seeking damages for his conviction and imprisonment as well as damages for burn injuries he received as a result of the fire. He claimed that his suit differed from *Cole* in that he was innocent of the crime because he suffered from diminished mental capacity at the time of the incident. The court rejected his claim, noting that the diminished-capacity claim was not a defense to a felony murder in the circumstances of this case.

In the *Cole* and *Veverka* cases the plaintiffs killed other people and then attempted to persuade the courts that they themselves were the real victims. Instead of seeking to compensate society, these plaintiffs wanted to get paid for their criminal acts. Fortunately, courts have properly ruled that the *Tarasoff* precedent has no application in these cases.

AIDS AND THE DUTY TO PROTECT

Acquired Immune Deficiency Syndrome (AIDS) is perhaps the most dangerous epidemic of the 20th century. Any "magic bullet" cure or vaccine for AIDS is decades away. The Human Immunodeficiency Virus (HIV), the precursor of AIDS, is most commonly transmitted through intimate sexual contact (especially unprotected anal intercourse), intravenous drug use, or in utero from mother to child. As of 1992 about 250,000 Americans have had AIDS including over 100,000 who have already died from AIDS. In addition, about 2 to 2.5 million Americans have the HIV infection and will develop AIDS in the next decade. By the end of the decade at least 1% of the American population will carry the HIV or have AIDS.

The spread of AIDS has led psychotherapists to worry about a situation where, in the course of treatment, patients may disclose that they have tested HIV positive. The patients may also reveal that they have identifiable sexual or drug-sharing partners who are not aware of their infections. Although psychotherapists have a responsibility to treat HIV-positive patients with compassion and understanding, they cannot ignore the threat to the public.

However, the laws with HIV-positive patients may differ considerably from that with patients who threaten to assault others. Psychotherapists in some states are prohibited from warning identifiable victims of persons who are HIV positive. As it pertains to a "duty to protect," psychotherapists need to consult authorities in their state and need to be aware that confidentiality laws concerning HIV-positive patients are continually changing.

Fortunately, effective psychotherapy can reduce the threat to the public and help patients as well. As with patients who pose a danger to assault others, sound clinical judgment can reduce the need for tortuous legal reasoning later. This section will review some of the legal/clinical issues to consider when treating patients who carry the HIV.

It is often difficult to assess the risk to others when dealing with HIV. Research has not identified all the risk factors involved in HIV transmission, so psychotherapists cannot be given absolute guidelines that apply in all situations. However, it is known that casual contact, even living together, will not lead to AIDS transmission. Transmission cannot occur through food, urine, or insect bites. Isolated reports of transmission through kissing, human bites, tattoos, or acupuncture have been made, but not confirmed (Castro et al., 1988). Persons who only live with the HIV-positive patient have no reason to fear for their health.

In contrast to casual contact, sexual contacts and sharing needles are primary modes of HIV transmission. The determination of whether the patient is engaging in high-risk sexual behavior is perhaps the most challenging part of the psychotherapist's task. Psychotherapists need to obtain a detailed and accurate description of their patients' sexual behavior. Failure to do so would provide insufficient or inaccurate information upon which to conduct psychotherapy.

Unprotected anal intercourse is always high-risk behavior, whether done with same-sex or different-sex partners. Vaginal-penile transmission of HIV can occur, although the rate of transmission is much lower than with anal intercourse.

Some HIV-positive patients engage in "safe sex," but have not notified their partners of their infection. Unfortunately, sex with an HIV-positive partner is never completely safe. Hearst and Hulley (1988) estimated that one-time penile-vaginal intercourse with one partner using a condom has a 1 in 5,000 infection risk, but 500 such encounters have a 1 in 11 risk. A one-time penile-vaginal encounter with one person without using a condom has a 1 in 500 infection risk, but 500 such sexual encounters have a 2 in 3 risk. The overall potential harm from HIV infection is greater if the potential victim is a woman of child-bearing age because 40% to 50% of infants born to HIV-positive mothers acquire the HIV infection in utero, through contact with maternal blood during delivery, or through breast-feeding (Friedland & Klein, 1987).

Reports of transmission through fellatio or cunnilingus have been made, although the risk of transmission is considerably lower than with vaginal intercourse. Some experts believe that the rates of transmission through oral sex are so low that it should be considered a safe-sex practice. Others, however, disagree (Kelly & St. Lawrence, 1988).

Transmission risks should consider co-factors, such as the presence of other sexually transmitted diseases that increase the likelihood of infection presumably through visible or microscopic lesions in the urethral, vaginal, or penile area (Quinn et al., 1988). The infectiousness of the host, which appears to increase over time, and the general health of the potential recipient may be other possible co-factors.

All HIV-positive patients should be considered potentially infectious regardless of whether or not they engage in "safe sex." Although barrier contraceptives can reduce the risk of infection (Condoms for Prevention of Sexually Transmitted Diseases, 1988), all partners should make an informed decision about continued sexual practices. The vulnerable partners should make the final decision as to whether to continue sexual relations, engage in only completely safe sex such as parallel or mutual masturbation, or discontinue the sexual relationship completely.

Anecdotal reports suggest that effective psychotherapy can encourage many HIV-infected persons to reveal their infection voluntarily to identifiable others (Howe, 1988; Perry, 1989). The patients who place others at risk usually have some conflict about their behavior. Discussing high-risk behaviors within psychotherapy may be a sign of concern for others that can be mobilized.

Unfortunately, a few patients may claim that they will engage in sexual activity with the purpose of infecting others or without regard for the possibility of disease transmission. This reaction may be a phase of dealing with the fatal nature of the disease and not represent a willful intention to harm others. Just as a verbal threat to assault a foreseeable third person may represent "blowing off steam," so the threat to infect others may reflect a momentary outburst of anger.

How should psychotherapists respond when dealing with HIV-dangerous patients who refuse to change their behaviors? Even in states which allow the application of *Tarasoff*, the *Tarasoff* court said, "a therapist should not be encouraged routinely to reveal such threats [of imminent physical danger] . . . unless such disclosures are necessary to avert danger to others" (p. 347). Neither the *Tarasoff* decision nor clinical judgment suggests indiscriminate reporting of the disease. A premature or inaccurate report of an HIV infection would cause those within psychotherapy to withhold information or terminate treatment prematurely. Unless these patients have incorporated a moral imperative to protect others, they may engage in high-risk activities with other unidentified or unidentifiable persons. Thus, the warning would lead to no overall improvement in the public safety.

When sexual partners engage in less risky practices, the danger of infection is not immediate. The psychotherapists have more time to persuade patients to disclose the infection to their partners voluntarily. But, if the risk of transmission is high, psychotherapists should make the patients' voluntary disclosure of their HIV status a more immediate focus of therapy.

Clinical experience with potentially assaultive psychiatric patients provides guidelines for psychotherapists if they believe warning is clinically and legally indicated. Potentially assaultive patients respond better when the psychotherapists speak openly about their concerns for endangered third parties. Warnings should be made, if at all possible, with the patients' consent or with the patients present. The psychotherapist can offer to make a phone call with the patient present, or have the patient present when the psychotherapist discusses the situation with the sexual partner. The openness helps reduce the suspicion about what might have been said and may reduce the harm to the psychotherapeutic relationship. Research has found that when psychotherapists made disclosures with the patients' knowledge or consent, the patients were much more likely to continue in treatment (Beck, 1982).

Several states have "partner notification" programs where trained state employees will notify the partners at the request of the patient. The psychotherapist or the patient can consider using the partner notification system instead of warning the intended victim directly.

How should psychotherapists treat patients who desire to change their sexual habits? Fortunately, Kelly (Kelly & Murphy, 1992; Kelly & St. Lawrence, 1988; Kelly et al., 1989) and others (e.g., Franzini et al., 1990) have developed promising treatment programs for homosexual men who want to change their high-risk behaviors. These studies rely on a combination of communications training, social support, stimulus control, cognitive restructuring, and education. The outcome appears encouraging and follow ups show that progress can be sustained, although relapse should be anticipated.

As with other dangerous patients, it is important to document treatment decisions. We encourage consultation with colleagues who are knowledgeable about sexual behavior, AIDS, or the HIV infection.

CLINICAL MANAGEMENT IN LIGHT OF *TARASOFF*

No court has specifically rejected the *Tarasoff* doctrine as a legal principle, although a few jurisdictions have elected not to apply it in the case presented to the court. As of 1987, several states (e.g., California, Georgia, Iowa, Kansas, Michigan, Minnesota, Nebraska, New Jersey, Oregon, Vermont, Wisconsin) and several federal district courts have found, or stated that under other circumstances they would find, a duty to protect third parties. Psychotherapists in all jurisdictions are advised to function as if the duty exists. Although the wide acceptance of the duty to protect, and its infrequent expansions to unnamed victims and to property damage, have increased the potential liability for therapists, the potential is rarely realized. Beck (1987) concluded from his extensive review of these duty-to-protect cases that therapists rarely have been found liable for failure to carry out the duty to protect, and in all but one of these cases, the courts concluded that the defendant had also failed to exercise reasonable care. Only in *Davis v. Lhim* (1983) did the court find failure to protect as the only basis for liability. Consequently, except for *Davis*, psychotherapists could have been found negligent without the *Tarasoff* doctrine.

Psychotherapists are now obligated to exercise professional judgment about potential violence and to take appropriate action based on that assessment. Some guidelines are now available for psychotherapists which can substantially reduce their risks when assessing and treating patients.

The guidelines are generic risk-management techniques which can be modified to apply to psychotherapists who are treating patients who are dangerous to themselves or others. The generic risk-management techniques include continuing education, external feedback, use of protocols, consultation, and accurate documentation.

Most dangerous patients are seen in specific and predictable kinds of settings. Dealing with dangerous adult patients is more likely to occur to psychotherapists who work in inpatient settings, because hospitalization is one of the preferred interventions with persons with serious mental illnesses who threaten others. Dealing with abusing parents is more likely to occur in outpatient clinics which specialize in the treatment of children. Psychotherapists who work in these settings can prepare themselves through continuing education courses, tutorials, or supervision to have the up-to-date skills in dealing with their particular client population.

In addition, psychotherapists in all settings should place themselves in a situation where their behavior is always being monitored or evaluated. This may include participation in a peer consultation group, use of patient satisfaction forms, evaluation of patient responses on standardized psychological tests, or some other mechanism designed to protect the psychotherapists from illusions of invincibility or freedom from error.

It is advisable to develop protocols for difficult patients. These protocols might include, for example, a predetermined structured interview for patients who threaten to harm others, a depression inventory for patients who have serious suicidal thoughts, or a parenting inventory for suspected child abusers. Although these instruments cannot replace clinical judgment, they can be important tools to support the clinician's decision concerning patient management.

Consultation should be an ongoing part of the work experience of every psychotherapist. In addition, psychotherapists should receive special consultations for every patient who appears to threaten others. Courts tend to give weight to consultations when assessing the level of care provided to the patient.

Finally, psychotherapists should record the assessment and treatment options carefully. They should describe in the patient's file the management options that have been considered. These records may be invaluable if the therapist's decisions are ever called into question (Soisson et al., 1987).

These generic guidelines can be helpful to psychotherapists who have to make decisions concerning the optimal manner in which to deal with life-endangering patients. By following these guidelines, psychotherapists will be more likely to make the optimal decisions concerning the assessment of and intervention with dangerous patients.

When making clinical decisions, psychotherapists need to distinguish between a duty to *assess* violence according to a reasonable standard of care and a duty to *predict* violence. The professional literature documents that therapists are imperfect in predicting violence (Monahan, 1984), and, except for *Davis*, courts have not found therapists liable for a failure to predict. Rather, the courts have found therapists negligent for failure to exercise due care in assessing potential for violence or for failure to act to protect third parties when the therapist determined that the patient was potentially violent. In this light, the *Tarasoff* doctrine does not necessarily impose an unwieldy burden on psychotherapists.

Clinicians can greatly reduce their vulnerability to lawsuits by understanding the *Tarasoff* principles and by exercising sound clinical judgment. The *Tarasoff* doctrine, if properly applied by the courts, is not likely to interfere with professional judgment. Appelbaum (1985) has encouraged psychotherapists to follow a three-stage procedure in analyzing their *Tarasoff* obligations. These stages are (a) identifying the procedures required to assess the degree of danger, (b) selecting the most appropriate intervention, and (c) implementing it. Liability may occur because of faulty behavior at any one of these three stages.

The first step requires that psychotherapists acquire information relevant to their evaluation of the potential for dangerousness. The *Tarasoff* court did not require psychotherapists to disclose every idle fantasy of harming others. On the contrary, the *Tarasoff* court stated: "A therapist should not be encouraged routinely to reveal such threats . . . unless such disclosures are necessary to avert danger to others" (p. 347).

A verbal threat alone is not sufficient to make the determination of imminent dangerousness, any more than a verbal threat of suicide means that a suicide attempt is imminent. The psychotherapist must use the procedures required to make a reasonable assessment. This means that the psychotherapist should explore personality dynamics, background of violent behavior, access to lethal weapons, the patient's relationship to the intended victims, and prior treatment.

Conversely, the absence of threat does not necessarily rule out the possibility of imminent dangerousness. The *Jablonski* court held that the failure of the aggressor specifically to threaten the victim does not exonerate the psychotherapist from failure to assess dangerousness. Instead, the court believed that a reasonably prudent psychotherapist would have acquired previous treatment records that would have revealed a background of dangerous behavior.

The second stage delineated by Appelbaum is the selection of the appropriate intervention. The *Tarasoff* court did not consider warning the intended victim as the only therapeutic response when danger arises. Instead, the psychotherapist may consider other procedures to reduce potential violence, including addressing the patient's anger as part of the psychotherapy, increasing the frequency of sessions, incorporating other parties into the treatment, asking the patient to relinquish any weapons, and instituting a treatment contract that asks the patient to avoid the potential victim or to contact the therapist when hostile urges increase. If these strategies seem insufficient, the psychotherapist may consider initiating an involuntary commitment or notifying the police. Indeed, cases have been presented in which warning the intended victim was a meaningless gesture, unnecessarily harmed the psychotherapeutic relationship, or may even have precipitated violence.

Wexler (1980) has suggested the option of having the potential victim participate in therapy. He believes that victims sometimes unknowingly precipitate the violence against themselves. To the extent that this is true, the therapist should attend to the pathological relationship between the patient and the potential victim rather than to the individual patient. Often the potential victim is a family member, lover, or close friend.

Roth and Meisel (1977) have suggested that social or environmental manipulations may reduce the risk of danger. For example, the psychotherapist can ask patients to rid themselves of lethal weapons. They believe that the psychotherapist must be frank with patients who speak seriously of harming others, and that the psychotherapist should inform the patient of the limits of confidentiality if serious threats continue. If the psychotherapist decides to warn a potential victim, Roth and Meisel suggest attempting to obtain the patient's consent first and, if possible, making the warning in the patient's presence. Such actions allow for consideration of the future of psychotherapy with the patient.

Beck (1982) studied the effects of making a warning upon the psychotherapeutic relationship. Although the sample size was small and the sampling was limited to psychiatrists in the Boston area, the study's conclusion supported Roth and Meisel's clinical intuition. "In every case in which a warning was warranted and discussed ahead, there was either a positive impact on therapy or no impact was apparent. However, if either the warning was not discussed ahead or was not warranted, then the impact was negative in four of five cases" (p. 194). Other case reports support Roth and Meisel's conclusions (e.g., Wulsin, Bursztajn, & Guthiel, 1983).

Appelbaum's final stage involves the appropriate implementation of the treatment decision, which is essential because an unimplemented plan is of no benefit. The *Tarasoff* case provides an example of failure at stage three. Dr. Moore had completed the first two stages of the three-stage procedure. He gathered enough data to make the determination of dangerousness and sought an appropriate intervention. The third stage, however, remained incomplete because the attempted commitment of Poddar failed. For reasons that are not clear from the case record, Dr. Moore's supervisor did not permit him to follow through on having Poddar taken into custody. It is valuable to seek consultation at each of these three stages with other mental health professionals, especially those who have expertise in dealing with potentially violent individuals.

STATUTORY REMEDIES TO *TARASOFF*

Many psychotherapists and professional associations have expressed concern about the potentially unreasonable expansion of the *Tarasoff* decision. They are concerned that courts may expand liability for patients who damage property, harm others without making a specific threat, or attack persons who are not readily identifiable. As a consequence, several states (California, Colorado, Indiana, Kansas, Kentucky, Louisiana, Massachusetts, Minnesota, Montana, New Hampshire, Ohio, and Utah) have enacted legislation that would limit liability to situations where the patient made a specific verbal threat to an identifiable victim.

For example, Minnesota's law states, in part, that the duty to protect does not arise "unless the patient or other person has communicated to the practitioner a specific serious threat of physical violence against a specific identified or identifiable potential victim" (Minnesota Statutes Annotated, West Supplement, 1987, p. 302).

Although such standards have merit, they may also overlook the typical steps that therapists should take to assess hostile patients. The assessment of dangerousness should not be restricted to a review of a specific concrete threat. Indeed, many verbal threats are merely "blowing off steam" by low-risk clients. Furthermore, under certain circumstances it is possible to make a determination of dangerousness in the absence of a specific directed threat. Instead, reasonable determinations of dangerousness are made from a combination of clinical and demographic variables of which verbal threats are only one possible factor.

Liability should be limited to cases in which the therapist failed to make a responsible assessment.

The second feature of many statutory remedies centers on how the duty is discharged. Minnesota's law states that "the duty is discharged by the practitioner if reasonable efforts are made to communicate the threat to the potential victim" (p. 302). Once again, reasonable practitioners may use many other appropriate interventions to discharge the duty before notifying the identified victim. The *Tarasoff* case itself acknowledged that the discharge of the duty could involve one of several actions, of which notifying the victim was only one possibility.

Finally, statutes should provide immunity for psychotherapists for reasonable actions taken to protect identifiable third parties from AIDS. The dangers to society from AIDS may well be greater than the danger posed by physically assaultive patients.

Liability should be assessed only when the therapist failed to act responsibly to protect the identified victim. Following closely a model presented by Beck (1987), we recommend the following statutory language:

> No monetary liability and no cause of action may arise against mental health service providers who are licensed or employed through a public mental health and mental retardation system who fail to predict, warn, or take precautions to provide protection from a patient's dangerous behavior toward others, including sexual behavior, if the providers have made reasonable professional efforts to assess the likelihood of such violence and those efforts have failed to yield evidence of imminent danger of harm against a clearly identified or reasonably identifiable victim or victims. Providers who determine that their patients pose a threat of danger to another shall discharge the legal duty to protect others by any professionally reasonable course of action including, but not limited to, communicating the threat to the victim or victims; notifying the appropriate law enforcement agency; arranging for the patient's voluntary hospitalization; petitioning for involuntary hospitalization; or developing a therapeutically indicated treatment plan with a reasonable likelihood of protecting the identifiable victim or victims.

OTHER LEGAL ISSUES
WITH DANGEROUS PATIENTS

This section will cover the lesser-known torts of abandonment and failure to refer. It will also survey the case law surrounding wrongful commitments.

ABANDONMENT

One of the fears that the *Tarasoff* decision raised was that psychotherapists might be tempted to prematurely terminate treatment with dangerous patients. Premature termination of treatment may place the therapist at risk of a charge of abandonment. The legal concept of abandonment has been applied primarily in medical malpractice cases, although its extension to psychotherapy would seem logical (VandeCreek, Knapp, & Herzog, 1987). Psychotherapists in private practice may refuse to accept a potential patient into treatment and limit the scope of their services at the outset of treatment. Psychotherapists, however, do not usually have the unqualified right to terminate an existing relationship unless the treatment is completed, the patient ends the relationship, or the psychotherapist recommends alternative services and assists the patient in finding them. A charge of abandonment has been upheld where a physician refused to continue treatment because of the patient's inability to pay for services, where the physician failed to recognize an illness that required treatment, and where the physician failed to provide sufficient coverage for patients during periods of vacation or other absences from the office.

The legal concept of abandonment could take two forms. First, abandonment would be unintentional in cases in which psychotherapists terminated treatment when they should have known that further treatment was needed, and the patient suffered harm or harmed another as a consequence of mental distress. Expert witnesses would be needed to determine the standard of reasonable care. Abandonment would be intentional in cases in which psychotherapists terminated or withheld treatment knowing that further care was needed. A lower standard of proof is required when a verdict of intentional abandonment is sought. The fact of termination itself, when the client clearly needed continuing care, might be sufficient to establish liability. In that case, expert witnesses would not be needed (Furrow, 1980). In addition, a plaintiff could claim *de facto* abandonment if the therapist failed to provide adequate access to treatment (Fulero, 1984).

Liability for the patient's care typically does not extend beyond the point of referral. For example, in *Brandt v. Grubin* (1974), a physician had referred his patient for psychiatric services. The patient subsequently committed suicide, but the referring physician was not liable. The court held that:

> A physician who upon an initial examination determines that he is incapable of helping his patient, and who refers the patient to a source of competent medical assistance, should be held liable neither for the actions of subsequent treating professionals nor for his refusal to become further involved with the case. (p. 89)

The potential application of the doctrine of abandonment to psychotherapy patients leaves many questions unanswered. For example, how does the doctrine of abandonment apply to community mental health centers that are not permitted to refuse services to new patients? How long must psychotherapists continue to treat patients who fail to pay their bills and appear to have no intention of ever doing so? Are psychotherapists required to continue to treat uncooperative, verbally abusive, and physically threatening patients?

Although no court has addressed the issues of abandonment with manipulative or abusive patients, Guthiel (1985) has suggested that it can be clinically indicated to restrict or refuse appointments with these patients at certain times. The duty to provide appointments should only refer to therapeutically indicated appointments. When psychotherapists believe it is indicated to limit or restrict appointments with impulsive, manipulative, or borderline patients, they should document treatment decisions carefully to avoid the appearance of neglect.

Clinicians who have worked with borderline or antisocial personalities know that vague or manipulative threats are common. It is hardly in the best interest of these patients to allow them to continue a self-defeating pattern of interpersonal behaviors. The doctrine of abandonment should not be used to coerce psychotherapists into reinforcing disruptive and self-defeating behaviors.

Although the parameters of the abandonment theory are not well-defined, it is clear that refusing to treat clients while they are a threat to themselves or others could constitute abandonment. After the immediate crisis has passed, psychotherapists can then take measures to collect bills, address the meaning of disruptive behaviors, or refer the patient elsewhere.

DUTY TO CONSULT OR REFER

Another consideration in the treatment of dangerous patients is the duty to refer or consult. Although no court has found liability for failure to refer a patient for psychotherapy, the court in *Peck v. The Counseling Service of Addison County* (1985) found the counselor negligent for, among other things, failure to consult with her supervisor or other therapists.

The medical malpractice literature provides precedents for a duty to refer. This duty arises when the psychotherapist determines, or should have determined, that the current treatments are unlikely to help the patient. This duty may become apparent in the first interview with the patient, or it may not become apparent until therapy has been conducted for many sessions. Verbal psychotherapy alone may not produce adequate benefits for some disorders such as schizophrenia or organic brain disorders, and in such cases nonmedical psychotherapists have a duty to refer the patient to a physician, preferably a psychiatrist. Other disorders, such as depression or anxiety, may respond either to psychotherapy or chemotherapy. Referral or consultation in these cases would be indicated when psychotherapists have exhausted their skills and the patient shows no reasonable likelihood of benefiting from continued treatment. The benefits of referral and consultation increase when the patient's potential for dangerousness is high. Failure to consult in these cases may make it appear to a court that the therapist was not alert to the patient's psychological needs.

At times a patient's condition may be so acute that a referral should be made directly to a hospital or other specialist for consideration for inpatient treatment. Under such emergency circumstances, patients may require assistance in completing the referral, and the referring therapist must be careful not to abandon the patient (Wise, 1979). Lion and Pasternak (1973) described a case in which a therapist was apparently unable to handle his fear of a threatening patient. The therapist escorted the patient to the emergency room of a local hospital, notified the clerk that he wished to admit the patient, and then left the patient sitting alone. The emergency-room psychiatrist found him 2 hours later. In retrospect, the referring therapist should have notified the emergency-room physician of the referral and provided relevant background information.

WRONGFUL COMMITMENT

A previous section detailed the liability that could occur from the failure to commit a patient. This section will consider wrongful or illegal commitments. Civil commitment decisions may place a psychotherapist in an apparent no-win situation. The failure to commit the patient may mean that a life is endangered. Conversely, the commitment of patients means a substantial deprivation of their freedom and an intrusion into their privacy. In addition to risks to the patients, psychotherapists may fear a legal risk to themselves through a malpractice suit or other tort action. Although professionals cannot always make commitment decisions with complete confidence, they are required to use reasonable judgment in making the decision. In addition, they are required to follow the letter of the law when they make the decision to commit a patient (Knapp & VandeCreek, 1987b).

Most courts hold that the physician-patient relationship which is a prerequisite for a malpractice suit does not exist when the professional first examines a prospective patient for the purpose of a civil commitment. Consequently, a malpractice suit is barred. A few courts, such as in New Jersey and New York, however, have held otherwise and allow malpractice actions in a civil commitment examination (*DiGiovanni v. Pessel*, 1970; *Kleber v. Stevens*, 1963). Of course, a court in any state would permit a malpractice action if psychotherapists initiated a civil commitment against patients with whom they already have a therapeutic relationship.

Aside from malpractice, psychotherapists who wrongfully commit patients could be liable for tort damages based upon other legal remedies, such as malicious prosecution, false imprisonment, or abuse of process (Knapp & VandeCreek, 1987b). Each of these legal remedies has certain prerequisites. A commitment proceeding must occur for malicious prosecution to exist. In addition, the proceeding must have resulted in a commitment, must have harmed the plaintiff, must have lacked probable cause, and must have been initiated with "malice" and not justice as a motive. False imprisonment refers to confinement within a restricted area, such as a hospital, by force or threat of force. Abuse of process occurs when the legal process is used to accomplish a purpose for which it was not designed and where external threats or acts are used (Prosser, 1971). For abuse of process to apply, a civil commitment would have to have been initiated for reasons other than treatment of mental illness or protection of society.

A court found false imprisonment in the case of *Eilers v. Coy* (1984), when the parents of a member of a religious cult held their son for deprogramming for more than 5 days. Although the court was sympathetic to the motives of the parents, it pronounced a verdict of false imprisonment because the parents held their son against his will with no reasonable means of escape, and did not follow the lawful procedures to initiate a civil commitment.

Courts also found false imprisonment charges in *Sukeforth v. Thegen* (1969). The court held the physician liable for false imprisonment when he failed to examine the patient as required by law, and then falsely swore that he had examined the patient and found him mentally ill and in need of confinement. Other courts have drawn similar conclusions when physicians have not examined patients as required by state law (e.g., *Lanier v. Salas*, 1985).

In contrast, a court failed to uphold a charge of false imprisonment in *Gonzalez v. State* (1985), when a man was involuntarily committed after he was found lying on subway tracks and could not explain why. The appellate court reversed a trial court which held that there was not enough evidence that the man was dangerous to himself to justify the commitment. Although the court exonerated the examining physician, it noted that courts will not automatically dismiss liability for false imprisonment just because the commitment was overturned. The question is whether the physician followed the prescribed procedures in determining and implementing a civil commitment.

The abuse-of-process tort occurred in the case of *Maniaci v. Marquette* (1971), when a university physician committed a college student. The 16-year-old student had made plans with her parents to leave school and had withdrawn money from the school bank. When questioned by the university officials as to her plans, however, she refused to give any details. The university officials committed her until they could reach her parents. They did not intend to provide psychiatric treatment, but only to detain her until they could speak to her parents.

The aforementioned cases were all successful because the professionals failed to comply with the letter of the law. By complying with the letter of commitment laws, mental health professionals become eligible for broad immunity provisions. For example, physicians who examine patients for a commitment may be immune because they are acting as agents of the court. This immunity holds even when the examination was made in a perfunctory manner or in bad faith. One rationale for the immunity is that the professional is only gathering information to be presented to the court. For example, in *Bailey v. McGill* (1957), a plaintiff charged that he received only a superficial examination before his commitment. The examination occurred while the patient was drugged, lasted only about 5 minutes, and consisted of only a few questions. The court, nevertheless, refused to find the physician liable because he acted in a judicial capacity.

Bailey contrasts with *Sukeforth v. Thegen* because the physician in *Sukeforth* did not perform any examination. The court in *Sukeforth* explained the extent of judicial immunity. The court acknowledged the inherent difficulties in such examinations and even went so far as to state that a brief examination may suffice when a traditional psychiatric examination becomes impossible. The court held that, nevertheless, "no physician acting in a quasi-judicial capacity can reasonably expect the protection of immunity if he had not seen fit to perform the elementary act by which he acquires jurisdiction over the person restrained" (p. 162).

APPLICATION OF SECTION 1983 OF THE CIVIL RIGHTS ACT

In addition to redress under the traditional torts, patients may sue psychotherapists for violation of rights guaranteed by the Constitution under the Civil Rights Act of 1871. The act reads, in part:

> Every person who, under color of any statute, ordinance, or regulation ... of any State ... subjects ... any citizen of the United States ... to the deprivation of any rights, privileges or immunities secured by the Constitution and laws shall be liable to the party injured in an action at law.

Because the relevant portion of the law appears in Section 1983 of Title 42 of the United States Code, it is referred to as Section 1983.

The act was popularly called "the Ku Klux Klan Act," and was enacted to control terrorist activities against black Americans following the emancipation of the slaves. The Congressional debates about this act were replete with references to the ruthless vigilante acts of the Klan and the failure of state governments to protect former slaves from the Klan. Congress wanted not only to attack the Klan, but also to prod those state officials who were unwilling to enforce laws against the Klan. The act allows aggrieved citizens to file complaints in federal courts to receive the protection of the 14th Amendment, which guarantees due process of law to all citizens.

Congress did not consider the application of the act to involuntary commitment to mental institutions when the law was enacted. The law, nevertheless, has been applied to that area. For Section 1983 to apply, the plaintiff must demonstrate that the mental health professional acted "under the color of the law" or in an official capacity. In addition, the plaintiff must prove that the professional acted in bad faith and violated constitutionally protected rights.

In *Dick v. Watonwan County* (1984), two alcohol counselors detained the parents of a 15-year-old girl who claimed that her parents were severely alcoholic. The girl had approached her guidance counselor with the request that she be placed in foster care. The guidance counselor had referred Miss Dick to two alcohol counselors. Miss Dick told those workers that her parents were endangering her life through their drunken behavior and that her father often drove after drinking. She claimed that her mother had vomited blood after drinking, that her parents often abused each other physically, and that her mother had threatened her father with a knife during a recent domestic altercation. On the basis of this information, the alcohol counselors initiated a commitment against Mr. and Mrs. Dick. They never attempted to contact the girl's sister to verify the reports, nor did they attempt to contact a social worker who had previously worked with the family. Finally, they did not have a physician's examination performed, as required by law.

Mr. and Mrs. Dick were apprehended on their way to a company Christmas party and confined in an alcohol-treatment facility, but they were soon released. At trial, it was learned that the statements on the petition were either completely erroneous or gross exaggerations. Miss Dick later admitted that her motive in trying to obtain foster care was to "get away with a lot more"; for example, staying up later at night. The court held that the alcohol counselors had deprived Mr. and Mrs. Dick of their civil rights by confining them without meeting the requirements of the law.

Although Section 1983 has expanded the liability of mental health professionals, it has not eroded the traditional protections. Professionals have the same immunity under Section 1983 as under state law if they act in good faith, or with a reasonable belief that they are acting properly. Finally, mental health professionals are not liable if they act in compliance with court orders, and they are not liable for unforeseen developments in constitutional law (Myers, 1973).

PROSECUTING PATIENTS

Inpatient therapists deal with many assaultive patients. The percentage of inpatients who are dangerous is higher in recent years, in part because most involuntary-commitment laws make dangerousness a prerequisite for commitment. In addition, hospitals now also admit patients committed by criminal courts.

Reid, Bollinger, and Edwards (1985) reported that about one-half of psychiatrists experience at least one serious assault during their careers. The vast majority of these acts result directly from the mental illness of the patients and need to be addressed in treatment. Inpatient treatment units should establish procedures by which these assaults may be foreseen and prevented. Of course, no unit can prevent all assaults, so the hospital should also have written guidelines for procedures to be used in handling patients after the assault occurs.

In addition, the treatment facility and the victim may bring criminal charges against assaultive patients. Although assaults are more likely to occur in inpatient units, employees and patients of outpatient centers may also be assaulted and may also initiate criminal charges.

Instituting criminal charges might be appropriate when therapists have exhausted their therapeutic options with the patient and the patient appears capable of distinguishing acceptable from unacceptable behavior (Hoge & Guthiel, 1987). In making the final decision about bringing criminal charges against a patient, the psychotherapist should consider the degree of internal control of the patient, the probability that the patient will repeat the violence, the willingness of the courts to prosecute, and the probable effect of legal proceedings against the patient on the long-term treatment relationship. For some patients, especially those with personality disorders who are resistant to treatment, prosecution may instill an understanding of the need for limits on their behavior. Hoge and Guthiel (1987) suggested that a weak therapeutic relationship and a poor prognosis increase the desirability of prosecution as part of a therapeutic strategy. They also caution that prosecution may deter the patient from seeking further services from mental health professionals.

Psychotherapists who treat assaultive patients often have to address countertransference reactions. Hoge and Guthiel (1987) suggest that if prosecution is being considered, then the treatment team should obtain a consultation from an independent psychotherapist whose judgment will not be affected by the treatment relationship.

MANDATORY REPORTING LAWS

Psychotherapists are often listed as reporters in mandatory reporting laws. All of these laws are based on the need to prevent harm to others and insure the public safety. Physicians are usually required to report gunshot wounds, sexually transmitted diseases, child abuse, and incompetent driving. Nonmedical psychotherapists are covered primarily by child-abuse reporting laws, although in recent years at least 20 states have passed adult-abuse reporting laws. Psychotherapists may also be included in the class of persons required to report incompetent drivers.

CHILD ABUSE

Psychotherapists encounter children who are endangered by the behavior of their parents or primary caregivers. In these situations, the mandated child-abuse reporting laws specify the psychotherapist's duty.

Child welfare advocates have succeeded in getting every state to adopt child welfare laws. These laws underwent major changes after the passage of P.L. 93-247, a federal law which made federal financial assistance contingent upon certain requirements, including mandating certain professionals to report suspected child abuse.

The state laws now typically require that professionals who deal with children report suspected child abuse when they encounter it in their professional duties. The list of mandated reporters includes physicians, psychologists, social workers, teachers, and other health and social service personnel.

The threshold for making reports is low. Reporters only need to suspect child abuse; they need not have proof. The intent of using a low threshold is to insure reporting of all potential cases and to leave the final determination with the child welfare agency. Psychotherapists are not asked to use their discretion about whether abuse actually did occur.

Privileged-communication laws are abrogated in all states for the initial report of child abuse. Privileged-communication laws for civil or criminal cases arising out of a report of child abuse, however, vary considerably according to the laws of individual states (Knapp & VandeCreek, 1987a; Weisberg & Wald, 1984).

The broadening of mandated reporting laws was followed by a substantial increase in the number of child-abuse reports, especially by groups of professionals who were not previously required to report (Sawyer & Maney, 1981). It is not known, however, how much of the increase is due to the mandated reporting provisions and how much is due to increased public awareness of the problem.

Incentives and Penalties Under Mandatory Reporting Laws. All child-abuse reporting laws seek to increase reporting through providing incentives and penalties. The incentives include immunity for reports made in good faith. The penalties include criminal fines and vulnerability to civil lawsuits for failure to make reports as required by law.

Federal law 93-247 required states to provide immunity to mandated reporters for reports made in good faith. The underlying rationale is that the state would prefer that psychotherapists err on the side of reporting rather than risk not reporting the case of an abused child. For a mandated reporter to incur liability for a false report, it would have to be proven that the psychotherapist knew that the report was not indicated but made it anyway. Such a fraudulent report would be extremely unlikely to occur and difficult to prove. Of course, there may be nonlegal consequences to an unfounded report, such as the loss of confidence in psychotherapists by their patients and consequent premature termination of psychotherapy.

The laws also provide criminal penalties against psychotherapists who fail to make the reports as required by law. It was intended, however, that these penalties would be rarely invoked, and reserved only for those who willfully disregarded the law (Note, 1979). As one commentator stated, "a penalty provision is both unenforceable and irrelevant, but it is felt that a *mandatory* reporting law must in theory be backed up by sanctions" (Maidment, 1978, p. 158). One of the supposed benefits of criminal sanctions is that professionals could use them as a justification for making the report (Maidment, 1978). One could imagine a situation where a supervisor would tell a nurse, who suspected child abuse, not to make the report because the hospital did not want to get involved. If the nurse pointed out that failure to report incurs criminal or civil penalties, however, the supervisor might become more cooperative.

In instances of flagrant disregard of the law, it may be easier to initiate criminal rather than civil sanctions, because criminal charges do not rely on a private party to initiate the legal action. In addition, public enforcement officials are required to pursue criminal sanctions even though private parties may be reluctant to seek a civil remedy.

Sometimes the statutes require that the mandated reporter have direct contact with the abused child before criminal penalties may be invoked. For example, in *State v. Groff* (1982), a psychiatrist was fined for failure to report suspected sexual abuse. The case was overturned, however, by an appeals court which held that the psychiatrist did not fall under the mandatory provision of the statute because he was not treating the child.

Furthermore, some states have provisions within their professional licensing laws that make the failure to fulfill a statutorily required duty a basis for disciplinary action, including suspension or revocation of a license to practice. The willful failure to report suspected child abuse would qualify under this provision of failing to fulfill a statutorily required duty.

In addition to the criminal penalties, civil suits have been initiated against mandated reporters who failed to report child abuse. Several states have legislated civil liability in this area. This is redundant, however, because a civil suit could be based on simple negligence; that is, the professional failed to adhere to the standard of care required by other similarly situated professionals, and the client (child) was harmed. In one case, a guardian *ad litem* initiated the case on behalf of an abused child who suffered permanent physical injury (*Landeros v. Flood*, 1976). The physician had failed to report or diagnose the battered-child syndrome, and the court ruled that he could be liable for damages if it could be shown that he had known of the abuse and still failed to make the report.

Most state statutes require that the failure to report be a "knowing and willful failure" for liability to accrue. Because failure to comply with a mandatory statute is negligence *per se*, this specific standard of liability may limit common-law liability. Most states that adopted this stricter standard of liability do not want to penalize honest mistakes in interpreting the ambiguous facts surrounding many child-abuse cases. This is an important provision because child-abuse reporting laws are often vague, and conscientious professionals may disagree on borderline cases concerning the presence or absence of child abuse. Consequently, criminal sanctions will apply only when reporters know that abuse is occurring and still fail to make a report (Note, 1979).

The failure to make a report as required by law is also an example of statutory negligence. Unlike other forms of negligence, the plaintiff only needs to prove that the statutorily required report was not made and that the child suffered as a consequence. Most courts presume that an individual failed to exercise due care when a statute is violated (Prosser & Keeton, 1985).

As noted previously, some statutes require that the mandated reporter have a direct relationship with the child before the duty to report is invoked. Seeing the child directly is often a prerequisite for learning about the abuse. Failure to see the child directly, however, does not necessarily provide immunity from prosecution for failure to report. Although no cases have been reported on this issue, it is conceivable that psychotherapists could be sued on the basis of the *Tarasoff* duty to protect (Besharov, 1986).

Recent Problems with Mandated Reporting. Child-abuse reporting laws have led to some new problems. Apparently unwarranted criminal sanctions against psychologists have been applied in at least three cases. In each case, the decision to prosecute was in the hands of a district attorney who may not have understood or considered the impact of such decisions on the family dynamics, the child welfare system, or the mental health professions. Fortunately, higher courts reversed these decisions in two of the three cases.

Although the complete facts are not available, it appears that these cases were "judgment calls" of abuse, and that reasonable professionals would likely disagree about whether abuse actually occurred. One possible effect of criminal sanctions being applied in questionable cases of abuse may be to reduce the number of professionals who are willing to serve these families.

Criminal penalties should be applied against psychotherapists who knowingly and willfully fail to comply in reporting obvious cases of child abuse. This was one intent of including the criminal penalties. But the criminal penalties were not intended to be applied in nebulous situations against well-meaning psychotherapists who, using the standards of their profession, did not believe that abuse was occurring.

Clinical Management of Potential Abuse Cases. Psychotherapists need to take special care in making decisions regarding the reporting of child abuse. Psychotherapists need to adhere carefully to the letter of the law to avoid personal liability. There is no substitute for knowledge of these laws. For example, states define child abuse differently. The broad term child abuse refers to one of four conditions: nonaccidental injury, neglect of physical needs, sexual abuse, and emotional abuse. Although every state includes nonaccidental injury and neglect of physical needs within its definition of child abuse, not all states include the last two elements. Also, as noted previously, some states require that psychotherapists have direct contact with the child before the mandated duty to report is invoked. In other states the psychotherapists are required to report if they learn of the abuse indirectly, such as through the perpetrator who has sought psychotherapy.

How should psychotherapists proceed when they believe a report of child abuse is indicated and they are prepared to make a report? As with other potentially dangerous clients, it is important to document cases carefully. In borderline cases it is especially wise to document what decision was made and why, and to consult with other professionals (Soisson et al., 1987).

Making the report of suspected abuse may alienate the parents and harm or destroy the psychotherapeutic relationship. Preliminary data from work with life-endangering adults, however, suggest that it is often prudent to discuss the requirement to make the report with the clients, and to obtain their consent when possible (Beck, 1982). If at all possible, the family should call the child welfare agency themselves, or the psychotherapist can make the call with the family present. Although the report of abuse may harm the psychotherapeutic relationship, this effort to clarify what was done and why it was done may minimize any damage. Of course, most states allow for reports to be made anonymously. This may be indicated in some situations, although patients sometimes can guess the identity of the reporter.

The mandated reporting feature of the law may help the psychotherapist in these situations. Psychotherapists can explain that the law requires them to report suspicions of child abuse and that criminal penalties could be incurred from a failure to do so.

ADULT ABUSE

As of 1988, all 50 states had passed elder abuse legislation, 44 having reporting requirements (Salend et al., 1984; Wolf, 1988). The laws usually apply to any adults who are unable to care for themselves because of mental or physical incapacity. Despite the wide targeting, the laws are generally intended to protect elderly persons.

These laws were modeled after the child-abuse reporting laws, except that financial exploitation is often included as a category for making a report. Psychotherapists are included in most, but not all, of these state statutes. All states guarantee immunity from liability from civil or criminal charges that may arise from making a report. Some, but not all, states have penalties for failing to report adult abuse. Civil suits based on failure to fulfill a statutory duty, such as in child-abuse cases, would apply here also.

INCOMPETENT DRIVERS

The laws regarding incompetent drivers vary from state to state. Generally speaking, physicians are required to report patients who are incapable of driving because of epilepsy, severe mental illness, or medication side effects. The laws or regulations may include nonmedical psychotherapists within the purview of mandated reporters. Furthermore, physicians have a responsibility to notify drivers of potential side effects of medication which may reduce their ability to drive. Failure to notify the patient of potential side effects of medication, or failure to notify the bureau of motor vehicles when the patient is incapable of driving, may result in a successful lawsuit if the driver were to harm another person. For example, in *Gooden v. Tips* (1983), the court held that a physician was potentially liable for failing to warn the patient of side effects of medication which would affect his driving.

Although the presence of seizures may be relatively easy to diagnose, the degree of mental illness required to trigger the duty to notify is not always clear. We all know of situations where even normal people are "too upset to drive" because of a tense emotional situation. Nonetheless, most people, including mental health patients, know when they are too upset to drive, and society expects them to avoid driving in those situations. The duty to notify is invoked only when patients are disturbed to an extent that they are unable to determine whether they are too upset to drive, or when patients are taking medications that impair driving ability.

DISCLOSURES OF PAST CRIMES IN COURT

Psychotherapists may sometimes wonder if they could be required to testify in court concerning information that their clients reveal to them in therapy. In these situations, privileged-communication laws may apply.

Psychotherapists need to distinguish the terms confidentiality and privileged communication. Confidentiality is the general term referring to regulation of the release of client information. Privileged communication is a subsection of confidentiality that deals only with the admission of evidence into court. When privileged-communication laws apply, clients can prevent their psychotherapists from testifying about them in court. State law regulates privileged communications in state courts; federal law regulates privileged communications in federal courts. The United States, consequently, has 52 sets of privileged-communications laws: one for each state, the District of Columbia, and federal courts.

Privileged-communication laws differ from most rules of evidence because they can exclude evidence from the court. Normally the courts have access to all evidence. The common law (judge-made legal tradition) holds that "the public has a right to every man's evidence." All persons have a duty to testify because the proper administration of justice benefits all. Privileged-communication laws are an exception in English and American law because they withhold information from the courts (Cleary, 1984). Courts usually interpret these laws strictly because they run counter to the common-law tradition of admitting evidence into court. Usually every letter of the law must be met before the court will permit a privilege law to apply.

Privileged-communication laws are porous and have many exceptions and waivers (Knapp & VandeCreek, 1987a). The exceptions to the privilege can be found in common-law interpretations of the privilege as well as specific statutory exceptions. Every state waives the privilege in the civil proceedings arising out of reports of suspected child abuse or involuntary civil commitment hearings. In addition, some states have specific exceptions to the privilege in criminal cases. For example, in California, the privilege applies only to psychiatrists and psychologists in criminal cases. The patients of social workers, school psychologists, and marriage and family therapists have no privilege in criminal cases in California. In Virginia, the privilege applies only to civil cases; no protection is provided in criminal cases. Indiana makes an exception to the privilege in cases of homicide when the disclosure is directly relevant to the fact or immediate circumstances of the murder. These and other exceptions mean that psychotherapists cannot expect to be exempted from testifying about actions of their clients that fall under these exceptions. Psychotherapists are encouraged to become familiar with the appropriate privilege laws in their state.

The exact rules and exceptions of privileged-communication statutes are too complex and variable to be presented in detail here. Extensive review of privileged-communication statutes can be found elsewhere (DeKraai & Sales, 1982; Knapp & Vande-Creek, 1987a).

SUMMARY

Psychotherapists who work with dangerous patients face a complex task of balancing the need of the patient for psychotherapy against the need of society for safety. Psychotherapy requires confidentiality and trust, but on occasion, the psychotherapist may determine that confidential information may need to be disclosed to protect potential victims from harm or to enhance treatment. In some instances, such as when a patient requires involuntary commitment, the decision to share confidential information is easy to make. In other cases, such as when a patient threatens harm to a third party, the psychotherapist's decisions may be clouded by confusion over legal duties.

The legal intrusions into the mental health field have received extensive coverage in professional and popular literature. The threats to clinical practice, however, have been more apparent than real. Psychotherapists have been found liable for failure to protect in only a handful of cases. With one exception (*Davis v. Lhim*, 1983), courts have found liability only when the psychotherapist also breached the traditional duty to use reasonable care. *Tarasoff* and subsequent decisions have not resulted in extensive intrusions of legal duties into mental health care.

Psychotherapists who treat dangerous patients must assess carefully the threat of harm to the patient and to potential victims. The assessment of dangerousness can be distinguished from the prediction of dangerousness. Courts have generally not found liability when the assessment of dangerousness was carried out with reasonable care, even if, in hindsight, the psychotherapist made an error in judgment. In contrast, courts have found liability when the defendant failed to carry out a thorough assessment.

The primary criteria that courts have reviewed in establishing liability in cases involving dangerous patients have been foreseeability of danger, identifiability of victims, and the ability of the psychotherapist to protect the victims. The clearest instances of liability occur when the assessment of danger produces a past record of dangerous behavior, the patient identifies a victim, and the therapist is in a position to warn, or in other ways to protect, the victim. The question of liability becomes cloudy when any of these criteria are not clearly met. In all instances, however, the psychotherapist must proceed with good clinical judgment.

Several states have enacted statutes to clarify the boundaries of liability of psychotherapists for the management of dangerous patients. Statutory protection, however, should not be viewed as a panacea, nor as a protection of inadequate clinical practice. Rather, such statutes should hold the professional to a realistic standard of care, while providing redress for society against foreseeable violence.

REFERENCES

Abernathy v. United States, 773 F.2d 184 (8th Cir. 1985).

Allen, J., & Curran, J. (1988). Prevention of AIDS and HIV infection: Needs and priorities for epidemiologic research. *American Journal of Public Health, 78,* 394-410.

American Law Institute. (1966). *Restatement of the Law, Second, Torts.* St. Paul, MN: American Law Institute Publishers.

Appelbaum, P. (1985). Tarasoff and the clinician: Problems in fulfilling the duty to protect. *American Journal of Psychiatry, 142,* 425-429.

Appelbaum, P., & Meisel, A. (1986). Therapists' obligations to report their patients' criminal acts. *Bulletin of the American Academy of Psychiatry and the Law, 14,* 221-230.

Bailey v. McGill, 100 S.E.2d 860 (NC 1957).

Bates v. Denney, 563 So.2d 298 (La. App. 1 Cir. 1990).

Beck, J. C. (1982). When the patient threatens violence: An empirical study after Tarasoff. *Bulletin of the American Academy of Psychiatry and Law, 10,* 189-201.

Beck, J. C. (1987, March-April). The psychotherapist's duty to protect third parties from harm. *Mental and Physical Disability Law Reporter, 11,* 141-148.

Beigler, J. S. (1984). Tarasoff v. Confidentiality. *Behavioral Sciences & the Law, 2,* 273-288.

Bellah v. Greenson, 146 Cal. Rptr. 535 (App. 1978).

Besharov, D. (1986, August). Child abuse and neglect: Liability for failing to report. *Trial,* pp. 67-72.

Bradley Center v. Wessner, 287 S.E.2d 716 (Ga. App. 1982).

Brady v. Hopper, 570 F. Supp. 1333 (D. Colo. 1983).

Brandt v. Grubin, 329 A.2d 82 (N.J. Super. 1974).

Cain v. Rijken, 717 P.2d 140 (1986).

Carlino v. State, 294 N.Y.S.2d 30 (1968).

Castro, K., Lifson, A., White, C., Bush, T., Chamberland, M., Lekatsas, A., & Jaffe, H. (1988). Investigations of AIDS patients with no previously identified risk factors. *Journal of the American Medical Association, 259,* 1338-1342.

Clark v. State, 472 N.Y.S.2d 170 (A.D.3 Dept. 1984).

Cleary, E. (Ed.). (1984). *McCormick's Handbook on the Law of Evidence* (3rd ed.). St. Paul, MN: West.

Cole v. Taylor, 301 N.W.2d 766 (Iowa 1981).

Comiskey v. State of New York, 418 N.Y.S.2d 233 (1979).

Condoms for Prevention of Sexually Transmitted Diseases. (1988). *Journal of the American Medical Association, 259,* 1925-1927.

Currie v. United States, 644 F. Supp. 1074 (M.D.N.C. 1986).

Currie v. United States, 836 F.2d 209 (4th Cir. 1987).

Dalton v. State, 308 N.Y.S.2d 441 (Sup. Ct. N.Y. App. 1970).

Davis v. Lhim, 335 N.W.2d 481 (Mich. App. 1983).

DeKraai, M. B., & Sales, B. D. (1982). Privileged communications of psychologists. *Professional Psychology, 13,* 372-388.

Dick v. Watonwan County, 562 F. Supp. 1083 (D. Minn. 1984).

DiGiovanni v. Pessel, 260 A.2d 510 (N.J. 1970).

Dinnerstein v. United States, 486 F.2d 34 (1973).

Doyle v. United States, 530 F. Supp. 1278 (D. Cal. 1982).

Eilers v. Coy, 582 F. Supp. 1093 (D. Minn. 1984)

Fair v. United States, 234 F.2d 288 (5th Cir. 1956).

Fernandez v. Baruch, 244 A.2d 109 (N.J. 1968).

Franzini, J., Sideman, L., Dexter, K., & Elder, J. (1990). Promoting AIDS risk reduction via behavioral training. *AIDS Education and Prevention, 2,* 313-321.

Friedland, G., & Klein, R. (1987). Transmission of the human immunodeficiency virus. *New England Journal of Medicine, 317,* 1125-1135.

Fulero, S. (1984). The concept of client abandonment. *West Virginia Psychological Association Newsletter,* pp. 5-6.

Furrow, B. R. (1980). *Malpractice in Psychotherapy.* Lexington, MA: D.C. Heath.

Goldberg, R. (1987). Use of constant observation with potentially suicidal patients in general hospitals. *Hospital and Community Psychiatry, 38,* 303-305.

Gonzalez v. State, 488 N.Y.S.2d 231 (A.D.2 Dept. 1985).

Gooden v. Tips, 651 SW2d 364 (Tex. App. Tyler 1983).

Greenberg v. Barbour, 322 F. Supp. 745 (D. Pa. 1971).

Guthiel, T. (1985). Medicolegal pitfalls in the treatment of borderline patients. *American Journal of Psychotherapy, 142,* 9-14.

Hasenei v. United States, 541 F. Supp. 999 (D. Md. 1982).

Hearst, N., & Hulley, S. (1988). Preventing the heterosexual spread of AIDS: Are we giving our patients the best advice? *Journal of the American Medical Association, 259,* 2428-2432.

Hedlund v. Superior Court of Orange County, 669 P.2d 41, 191 Cal. Rptr. 805 (1983).

Hicks v. United States, 511 F.2d 407 (D.C. Cir. 1975).

Hirsch v. State, 168 N.E.2d 372 (1960).

Hofmann v. Blackmon, 241 So.2d 752 (Fla. App. 1970).

Hoge, S., & Guthiel, T. (1987). The prosecution of psychiatric patients for assaults on staff: A preliminary empirical study. *Hospital and Community Psychiatry, 38,* 44-55.

Howe, E. (1988). Ethical aspects of military physicians treating servicepersons with HIV/Part Three: The duty to protect third parties. *Military Medicine, 153,* 140-144.

Jablonski v. United States, 712 F.2d 391 (9th Cir. 1983).

Kaiser v. Suburban Transportation System, 65 Wash.2d 461, 398 P.2d 14 (1965).

Kamenar, P. D. (1984). Psychiatrist's duty to warn of a dangerous patient: A survey of the law. *Behavioral Sciences & the Law, 2,* 259-272.

Kelly, J., & Murphy, D. (1992). Psychological interventions with AIDS and HIV: Prevention and treatment. *Journal of Consulting and Clinical Psychology, 60,* 576-585.

Kelly, J., & St. Lawrence, J. (1988). *The AIDS Health Crisis.* New York: Plenum.

Kelly, J., St. Lawrence, J., Hood, H., & Brasfield, I. (1989). Behavioral interventions to reduce AIDS risk activities. *Journal of Consulting and Clinical Psychology, 57,* 60-67.

King, J. (1977). *The Law of Medical Malpractice.* St. Paul, MN: West.

Kleber v. Stevens, 241 N.Y.S.2d 497 (1963).

Knapp, S. & VandeCreek, L. (1983). Malpractice risks with suicidal patients. *Psychotherapy: Theory, Research and Practice, 20,* 274-280.

Knapp, S., & VandeCreek, L. (1987a). *Privileged Communications for Mental Health Professionals.* New York: Van Nostrand Reinhold.

Knapp, S., & VandeCreek, L. (1987b). A review of tort liability in involuntary civil commitment. *Hospital and Community Psychiatry, 38,* 648-651.

Landeros v. Flood, 551 P.2d 389 (Cal. 1976).

Lanier v. Salas, 777 F.2d 321 (5th Cir. 1985).

Leonard, J. B. (1977). A therapist's duty to potential victims: A nonthreatening view of Tarasoff. *Law and Human Behavior, 1,* 309-317.

Leverett v. State, 399 N.E.2d 106 (Ohio Ct. App. 1978).

Lion, J., & Pasternak, S. (1973). Countertransference reactions to violent patients. *American Journal of Psychiatry, 130,* 207-210.

Lipari v. Sears, 497 F. Supp. 185 (D. Neb. 1980).

Maidment, S. (1978). Reporting child abuse. *Current Legal Problems, 1978,* 150-175.

Maniaci v. Marquette, 194 N.W.2d 168 (Wisc. 1971).

Marzuk, P., Tierney, H., Tardiff, K., Gross, E., Morgan, E., Hsu, M. A., & Mann, J. (1988). Increased risk of suicide in persons with AIDS. *Journal of the American Medical Association, 259,* 1333-1337.

Matter of Estate of Votteler, 327 N.W. 759 (Iowa 1982).

Mavroudis v. Superior Court for County of San Mateo, 162 Cal. Rptr. 724 (App. 1980).

McCarthy, M. (1964). *The Group.* New York: Signet.

McIntosh v. Milano, 403 A.2d 500 (N.J. 1979).

Minn. Stat. Ann. 148.975 (West Supp. 1987).

Monahan, J. (1984). The prediction of violent behavior: Toward a second generation of theory and policy. *American Journal of Psychiatry, 141,* 10-15.

Moore v. United States, 222 F. Supp. 87 (D. Mo. 1963).

Myers, P. (1973). Right to relief under federal civil rights act of 1871 (42 U.S.C. 1983) for alleged wrongful commitment to or confinement in mental hospital. *American Law Reports-Federal, 16,* 440-498.

Note. (1979). Child abuse and neglect. *Villanova Law Review, 23,* 445-546.

Paradies v. Benedictine Hospital, 431 N.Y.S.2d 175 (App. Div. 1980).

Peck v. The Counseling Service of Addison County, 499 A.2d 422 (Vt. 1985).

Perr, I. (1985). Suicide litigation and risk management: A review of 32 cases. *Bulletin of the American Academy of Psychiatry and Law, 13,* 209-219.

Perry, S. (1989). Warning third parties at risk for AIDS: APA's policy is a barrier to treatment. *Hospital and Community Psychiatry, 40,* 158-161.

Prosser, W. (1971). *The Law of Torts.* St. Paul, MN: West.

Prosser, W., & Keeton, W. P. (1985). *Prosser and Keeton on the Law of Torts.* St. Paul, MN: West.

Quinn, T., Glasser, D., Cannon, R., Matuszak, D., Dunning, R., Kline, R., Campbell, C., Israel, E., Fauci, A., & Hook, E. (1988). Human immunodeficiency virus infection among patients attending clinics for sexually transmitted diseases. *New England Journal of Medicine, 318,* 197-203.

Reid, W., Bollinger, M., & Edwards, G. (1985). Assaults in hospitals. *Bulletin of American Academy of Psychiatry and Law, 13,* 1-4.

Ross v. Central Louisiana State Hospital, 392 So.2d 698 (La. App. 1980).

Roth L., & Meisel, A. (1977). Dangerousness, confidentiality, and the duty to warn. *American Journal of Psychiatry, 134,* 508-511.

Runyon v. Reid, 510 P.2d 943 (Okl. 1973).

Salend, E., Kane, R., Satz, M., & Pynoos, J. (1984). Elder abuse reporting: Limitations of statutes. *The Gerontologist, 24,* 61-69.

Sawyer, D., & Maney, A. (1981). Legal reform in child abuse reporting: A time series analysis. *Evaluation Review, 5,* 758-767.

Seligman, M. (1989). Research in clinical psychology: Why is there so much depression today? In I. Cohen (Ed.), *The G. Stanley Hall Lecture Series* (Vol. 9, 75-96). Washington, DC: American Psychological Association.

Semler v. Psychiatric Institute of Washington, 538 F.2d 121 (4th Cir. 1976).

Sharpe v. South Carolina Department of Mental Health, 315 S.E.2d 112, (S.C. 1984).

Sherrill v. Wilson, 653 S.W.2d 661 (Mo. 1983).

Skillings v. Allen, 173 N.W. 663 (Minn. 1919).

Soisson, E., VandeCreek, L., & Knapp, S. (1987). Thorough record keeping: A good defense in a litigious era. *Professional Psychology: Research and Practice, 18,* 498-502.

State v. Groff, 409 So.2d 45 (Fla. App. 1982).

Stone, A. (1976). The Tarasoff decision: Suing psychotherapists to safeguard society. *Harvard Law Review, 90,* 358-378.

Sukeforth v. Thegen, 256 A.2d 162 (Me. 1969).

Tarasoff v. Regents of the University of California, 13 Cal.3d 177, 529 P.2d 533 (1974), *vacated,* 17 Cal.3d 425, 551 P.2d 334 (1976).

Teasley v. United States, 662 F.2d 787 (D.D.C. 1980).

Thompson v. County of Alameda, 614 P.2d 728 (1980).

Underwood v. United States, 356 F.2d 92 (5th Cir. 1966).

VandeCreek, L., Knapp, S., & Herzog, C. (1987). Malpractice risks in the treatment of dangerous patients. *Psychotherapy, 24,* 145-153.

Veverka v. Cash, 318 N.W. 447 (Iowa, 1982).

Wagshall v. Wagshall, 538 N.Y.S. 2d 597 (A.D. 2 Dept. 1989).

Weisberg, R., & Wald, M. (1984). Confidentiality laws and state efforts to protect abused or neglected children: The need for statutory reform. *Family Law Quarterly, 18,* 143-212.

Wexler, D. (1980). Victimology and mental health law: An agenda. *Virginia Law Review, 66,* 681-711.

White v. United States, 780 F.2d 97 (D.C. Cir. 1986).

Wise, T. (1979). The responsibility of a referring psychiatrist. *Lawyer's Medical Journal, 7,* 207-211.

Wojcik v. Aluminum Company of America, 183 N.Y.S.2d 351 (1959).

Wolf, R. S. (1988). Elder abuse: Ten years later. *Journal of the American Geriatrics Society, 36,* 758-762.

Wulsin, L., Bursztajn, H., & Guthiel, T. (1983). Unexpected clinical features of the Tarasoff decision: The therapeutic alliance and the "duty to warn." *American Journal of Psychiatry, 140,* 601-603.

Add A Colleague To Our Mailing List . . .

If you would like us to send our latest catalog to one of your colleagues, please return this form.

Name:_____
(Please Print)

Address:_____

Address:_____

City/State/Zip:_____

Telephone:(_____)_____

I am a:

_____ Psychologist   _____ Mental Health Counselor
_____ Psychiatrist   _____ Marriage and Family Therapist
_____ School Psychologist   _____ Not in Mental Health Field
_____ Clinical Social Worker   _____ Other:_____

◆   ◆   ◆

Professional Resource Press
P.O. Box 15560
Sarasota, FL   34277-1560

Telephone #941-366-7913
FAX #941-366-7971

If You Found This Book Useful . . .

You might want to know more about our other titles.

If you would like to receive our latest catalog, please return this form:

Name:_____
(Please Print)

Address:_____

Address:_____

City/State/Zip:_____

Telephone:(_____)_____

I am a:

_____ Psychologist   _____ Mental Health Counselor
_____ Psychiatrist   _____ Marriage and Family Therapist
_____ School Psychologist   _____ Not in Mental Health Field
_____ Clinical Social Worker   _____ Other:_____

◆　　　◆　　　◆

Professional Resource Press
P.O. Box 15560
Sarasota, FL 34277-1560

Telephone #941-366-7913
FAX #941-366-7971

TAB/1/97